ISSUE 21, JUNE 2024

AUSTRALIAN FOREIGN AFFAIRS

Contributors

Emma Connors was the *Australian Financial Review*'s South-East Asia correspondent from October 2019 until mid-2023, and covered Indonesia's 2024 presidential election for the *AFR*.

Ian Hall is a professor of international relations at Griffith University and an honorary fellow of the Australia India Institute at the University of Melbourne.

Bart Hogeveen is deputy director for Cyber, Technology, and Security at the Australian Strategic Policy Institute.

Evan A. Laksmana is senior fellow for Southeast Asia Military Modernisation and editor of the *Asia-Pacific Regional Security Assessment* at the International Institute for Strategic Studies.

Sarah Percy is associate professor of international relations at the University of Queensland. Her most recent book is *Forgotten Warriors: A History of Women on the Front Line*.

Gatra Priyandita is an analyst at the Australian Strategic Policy Institute.

Steven Ratuva is a distinguished professor, a pro-vice chancellor and director of the Macmillan Brown Centre for Pacific Studies at the University of Canterbury.

Sam Roggeveen is the director of the Lowy Institute's International Security Program and author of *The Echidna Strategy: Australia's Search for Power and Peace*.

Maria Monica Wihardja is a visiting fellow at ISEAS–Yusof Ishak Institute and an adjunct assistant professor at the National University of Singapore. She was an economist at the World Bank and the Nikkei Asian Scholar in 2023.

Australian Foreign Affairs is published three times a year by Australian Foreign Affairs Pty Ltd. Publisher: Morry Schwartz. Editor-in-chief: Erik Jensen. ISBN 978-1-76064-4321 ISSN 2208-5912 Subscriptions – 1 year print & digital auto-renew (3 issues): $49.99 within Australia incl. GST. 1 year print and digital subscription (3 issues): $59.99 within Australia incl. GST. 2 year print & digital (6 issues): $114.99 within Australia incl. GST. 1 year digital only auto-renew: $29.99. Payment may be made by MasterCard, Visa or Amex, or by cheque made out to Schwartz Books Pty Ltd. Payment includes postage and handling. To subscribe, fill out the form inside this issue, subscribe online at www.australianforeignaffairs.com, email subscribe@australianforeignaffairs.com or phone 1800 077 514 / 61 3 9486 0288. Correspondence should be addressed to: The Editor, Australian Foreign Affairs, 22–24 Northumberland Street, Collingwood, VIC, 3066 Australia Phone: 61 3 9486 0288 / Fax: 61 3 9486 0244 Email: enquiries@australianforeignaffairs.com. Editor: Jonathan Pearlman. Deputy Editor: Julian Welch. Associate Editor: Chris Feik. Design: Peter Long. Production Coordination: Marilyn de Castro. Typesetting: Tristan Main. Cover photograph: Lukas Coch / AAP. Printed in Australia by McPherson's Printing Group.

Editor's Note

THE JAKARTA OPTION

On 14 December 1995, Australian prime minister Paul Keating held a press conference at Parliament House to announce a landmark security deal with Indonesia, which had somehow been kept secret despite eighteen months of planning.

The deal was a diplomatic breakthrough for Canberra, which, as Keating told reporters, did not view Indonesia as a threat, believing instead that a "sound strategic relationship" was crucial to Australia's security. And it was a breakthrough for Indonesia, a staunchly non-aligned nation that had not previously committed to this type of joint security agreement.

Nine years later, Keating's successor, John Howard, delivered his own Indonesia surprise. Two weeks after the devastating Boxing Day tsunami, in which more than 150,000 Indonesians died, Howard visited Jakarta and revealed that he was providing $1 billion in aid – an amount that stunned both countries.

The move, as Howard later acknowledged, was not merely a response to the disaster but "a sign to the rest of the world of how important Indonesia was to Australia". "The magnitude and symbolism of the tsunami relief – they did a lot to improve relations and put the relations between the two countries on about as sound a footing as they can ever be," he told *The Australian* in 2014.

Less than two years after the aid announcement, Australia and Indonesia signed the Lombok Treaty, a far-reaching security deal that effectively replaced the 1995 agreement, which had been scrapped by Jakarta in 1999 as relations frayed ahead of Timor-Leste gaining independence.

Australia's two security deals with Indonesia have reshaped the neighbouring nations' relationship. Though business and cultural links between the pair remain pathetically thin, and despite a paucity of understanding or curiosity on both sides, the strategic relationship is no longer guided by suspicion but by cooperation. But two changes in Asia are raising questions about whether the current relationship needs to make its next leap.

First, the rise of China, and the threat of conflict as its rivalry with the United States intensifies, poses risks that are forcing Australia and Indonesia to take new security steps, such as acquiring nuclear-powered submarines or edging away from non-alignment. A move by the two countries towards the ultimate form of security assurance – a treaty in which they agree to defend each other from an attack by a foreign state – looks less and less radical.

The other reason Canberra's ties with Jakarta are set to evolve is that Indonesia – the world's fourth-most populous country – is expected to become a major international power. But its military capability and role on the global stage will depend on whether it fulfils its plan to become one of the world's top five economies in the next twenty years. (It is currently ranked sixteenth; Australia is twelfth.)

For Australia, it will be crucial to understand Indonesia's economic and political trajectory, especially as it shifts to a new president in October 2024. Unlike President Joko Widodo, a former carpenter, Prabowo Subianto is a former general whose record includes alleged oversight of tortures and kidnappings. But Prabowo is also a veteran politician who has made various alliances of convenience. Canberra's ties with Jakarta will hinge on whether Prabowo turns out to be the smiling grandparent of his winning election campaign or an ultranationalist strongman – or something else altogether.

But Keating's and Howard's legacies also offer an important lesson about the Australia–Indonesia relationship: surprises are possible. Achieving deeper ties will hinge on the types of leaders in Canberra and Jakarta, and on whether they are willing to contemplate or risk further advances. And it will hinge on whether, or how quickly, stability in the region deteriorates: Russia's invasion of Ukraine in 2022, for instance, prompted Sweden and Finland to abandon decades of neutrality and join NATO, and led Germany to overhaul its post–World War II pacifism.

Much has changed in the region since Keating's 1995 press conference. But it remains true that Canberra must forge closer ties with Jakarta to find security in Asia. To do so, Australia will need to properly understand Indonesia's evolving politics and economy, and the opportunities for uncovering – or creating – the two nations' next great leap forward.

Jonathan Pearlman

UNITED FRONT

Australia needs a military alliance with Indonesia

Sam Roggeveen

The moment has arrived for Australia to consider what would be its most ambitious and important foreign-policy initiative of the century so far: the forging of a military alliance with Indonesia. "Alliance" is a jarring word. For Indonesia, it sits uneasily alongside its tradition of non-alignment. For Australia, it is a term that we have only ever associated with English-speaking great powers. There is also an understandable fear that such an alliance will provoke confrontation. But the agreement proposed here is not a militarist fantasy advocating an arms race with Beijing. It is not about "securitising" the relationship with Jakarta or bringing a new Cold War to South-East Asia or drawing Indonesia into the Western fold. In fact, the alliance described here is designed expressly to move military matters to the background of regional relations, and to avoid South-East Asia becoming a theatre for a United States–China rivalry.

But until Australia and Indonesia forge a partnership that makes it impossible for China to further its ambitions through military coercion, any constructive agenda for the region will remain hostage to Beijing's ambitions. Military power is critical to the future regional order not because that order will necessarily be decided on the battlefield but because the capability and willingness to resist military coercion will be decisive. The alliance proposed here is designed to neutralise China's growing capacity to project power over the seas, so that social, economic and environmental progress can take precedence.

China shows no evidence of being an expansionist power like Nazi Germany or imperial Japan, but it does aim to become the dominant power in Asia. And what does domination mean? It will rest on a belief, shared by China's friends and foes alike, that Beijing is strong enough to impose its will at any moment. It is not colonialism or direct political command, but acquiescence that comes from the knowledge that the great power can crush dissent should it ever need to do so.

Such dominance is based ultimately on military power, the ability to inflict enough pain on an adversary to dissuade them from resisting. When a great power knows that its smaller adversaries lack the means to resist such pressure, it has a greater scope to achieve its ambitions through military coercion. A militarily dominant nation may never need to issue direct threats because weaker states will avoid putting themselves in a position where they could face the humiliation of yielding to them. Without being used, military power will have served the purpose of constraining the smaller power.

This logic has its limits. Most disputes between states are settled well below the military threshold, and other forms of power – particularly economic – can be so omnipresent as to remove the necessity for military coercion. But vulnerability to military power does leave states with less space to exercise sovereignty, because they know the great power can always veto their decisions.

So Australia and Indonesia should aim to ensure that China can never dominate them militarily. To be clear, this doesn't mean they need to compete with China to become Asia's leading military power. That would be an impossible task: China already has the world's largest navy, if not the most capable. But there's a critical difference between leadership and dominance: the former means having the most and the best, but the latter means you can overpower any adversary without risking unacceptable costs. Dominance is a higher bar than leadership, and consequently it will be easier for Australia and Indonesia to prevent it. Nor will they need to match all aspects of China's massive military machine. The region we jointly inhabit is maritime in nature, and that means Indonesia and Australia can focus their alliance solely on blunting China's maritime power.

Maritime power

Luckily, China itself has given us a blueprint for how to do this.

The first phase of China's military modernisation process, from the early 1990s to the mid-2000s, was focused largely on developing defensive capabilities – that is, the ability to blunt an American fleet dedicated to the offensive use of maritime power. The capital ships of the US Navy – aircraft carriers, missile cruisers and amphibious vessels – were all devoted to a strategy that would give the US uninterrupted use of the oceans, in turn allowing it to project power ashore. China set itself the task of negating that capability by focusing its maritime modernisation almost exclusively on sinking ships. It did this by building an ever more deadly and far-reaching arsenal of anti-ship weapons mounted on coastal launchers, submarines, ships and aircraft. During the 1996 Taiwan crisis, the US Navy could sail aircraft carriers and amphibious ships through the Taiwan Strait as a demonstration of strength. The Americans were sailing less than 200 kilometres from the Chinese coast, secure in the knowledge that if the crisis escalated to war, these ships could defend themselves against China's meagre capabilities. Nowadays, the US could not guarantee the safety of its ships out to 4000 kilometres from China's coast, this being the approximate range of China's DF-26B, the world's first ballistic missile designed to hit ships at sea. The US is not prevented from sailing warships within this boundary, but it would have to fight its way in against sharply rising odds. The whole point of China's strategy is for the US to judge that it cannot risk taking its valuable ships close enough to strike.

China would prefer that the US doesn't put up a fight

In the second phase of its military modernisation, China moved beyond a defensive maritime strategy to an offensive one. First came a series of relatively sophisticated frigates and destroyers. Then, in the late 2000s, unambiguous evidence of a Chinese aircraft carrier program. Today, China is turning out carriers, cruisers, destroyers and frigates rivalling any American or European design, but building them much more quickly.

This shift looked paradoxical: the first phase of China's modernisation was supposed to exploit a technological and economic imbalance between the offensive and defensive uses of force at sea – a 2016 RAND study said the average cost of defensive capability is about one-fiftieth of the cost of the offensive capability that it could neutralise in combat. Yet the second phase of China's modernisation seemed to deny the conclusions that had driven the first. China had convinced itself that large surface ships were obsolete, yet here it was building a costly surface fleet.

The most plausible explanation for this paradox is also the most worrying. China's maritime strategy, and specifically the ships it is building, give us a big clue about how it wants to exercise dominance in South-East Asia. Chinese leaders never tell us what they want, so their ambitions and intentions must be understood by inference and deduction. But this is not an entirely speculative exercise. We can be confident that an initiative as big as the naval ship-building program, which includes several giant aircraft carriers, has been agreed at the very highest levels of Chinese decision-making. It is thus a material expression of Chinese statecraft and national intent.

China learnt an important lesson from America's use of maritime power, particularly in the post–Cold War world: while the offensive use of maritime power was becoming more difficult and costly, that only applies when your adversary has sufficient defensive capabilities. The story of post–Cold War American maritime power, however, is one of taking on adversaries that have little or no defensive naval power: Panama, Grenada, Somalia, Iraq, Serbia, Afghanistan, Libya, Syria. In the absence of a rival that might contest America's command of the oceans, the US fleet had become a constabulary force used to project its maritime power onto land at little risk to itself. China has a similar ambition. It is building this offensive fleet not to take on the US but to police the regional order that Beijing wants to impose.

China can't be the uncontested leader of the Asian regional order while the United States is still around, so it will need to push the Americans out first, by force if necessary. That's what China's defensive fleet is for. Of course, China would prefer that the US doesn't put up a fight. It increasingly thinks of the US as a declining power, and its expectation may be that Washington simply gives up trying to match Beijing's military resources and ambition.

There's certainly evidence to back that up. The US failed to contest China's most brazen act of maritime expansion in the 2010s, when it built artificial islands in the South China Sea, thus effectively handing China control of these waterways without a fight. Nor has the US responded sufficiently to China's military expansion: Washington has modernised its forces in the Asia Pacific since the end of the Cold War and is now spreading them around new bases (including in Australia), but it hasn't substantially built up its forces. Beijing is betting that the US will eventually give up and go home.

The offensive fleet China is building is therefore not designed to take on the US but to inherit America's crown as the dominant maritime power in Asia. China is building a post-American navy.

Why Indonesia?

To understand why an Indonesia–Australia military alliance is necessary, we must imagine a post-American Asia in which China is striving to become the dominant power. This doesn't necessarily mean the US will be physically absent (although we shouldn't dismiss that possibility, especially under a second Trump presidency). But we do need to think about an America that is less motivated to defend its allies.

In such a world, Australia needs to find other partners. Why, among the options available, should we choose Indonesia? Japan is an obvious alternative candidate, but it's too far away. Any security threat against Japan will not threaten Australia's vital interests, and vice versa. That will inhibit each country's motivation to make sacrifices on behalf of the other. And mutual sacrifice is really at the heart of any alliance – an understanding that the parties will come to each other's aid not out of legal or moral duty but because it will damage their own vital interests if they fail to do so. That's the main reason Australia should favour Indonesia. If China were ever to be the dominant maritime power in South-East Asia, it would threaten Indonesia's interests as much as

Australia's, which means both are motivated to help each other. Indonesia and Australia share an overlapping strategic space, which each has a vital interest in defending.

But if geography is the determining factor, why not ally with Singapore, the Philippines or Thailand? Australia certainly should strive to improve defence relations with these countries, but none is an immediate neighbour, and none has Indonesia's size, stature or potential. Indonesia is already ASEAN's undisputed leader and the biggest economy in South-East Asia. It is the only country in the region with the population (275 million) and economic capacity to become a great power; on present economic trends, we will be thinking of Indonesia that way by mid-century. Because of its size, there's less risk that Indonesia will "bandwagon" with China. Laos and Cambodia are already on this path: they are weak states aligning with a stronger one on the basis that the costs of resisting will outweigh the benefits. Indonesia is unlikely to follow them.

Ukraine is demonstrating that smaller countries can nullify the maritime power of much larger adversaries

Bandwagoning is exactly what China is counting on in maritime South-East Asia. It wants to build a regional order of quiescent nations that, while remaining independent in their domestic affairs and maintaining armed forces of their own, will defer to Beijing on major strategic questions. The PLA Navy, and particularly its offensive fleet, will be the constabulary force used to police this order.

Defensive allies

It should therefore be clear what kind of military alliance Australia and Indonesia need to frustrate these ambitions: one devoted solely to the task of denying any foreign power dominance of maritime South-East Asia. China cannot be the dominant power and cannot constrain the independent decision-making of Indonesia and Australia if its maritime power is blunted, and the way to achieve that is to build capabilities that look very much like the defensive fleet China itself built in the first phase of its modernisation. That suggests a tight focus on the ability to find and sink ships, for which you need a comprehensive network of surveillance capabilities to monitor the seas, and a battery of missiles, torpedoes and mines that can neutralise seaborne threats. Such a force would avoid many traditional naval weapons, such as aircraft carriers, destroyers and amphibious vessels. It would employ nimble "shoot and scoot" platforms – aircraft, small surface vessels and diesel submarines – to monitor the oceans and launch weapons.

Australia can offer Indonesia much-needed help to develop a modern military focused on maritime power. During President Jokowi's decade in office, Indonesia has introduced only a handful of new naval combatants and combat aircraft. Its surveillance capabilities – essential for maritime denial strategy but challenging over vast distances – are also lacking. Australia has spent decades developing, building and modernising the Jindalee radar network, which can monitor air and sea movements over tens of thousands of square kilometres across Australia's north. Jindalee is now complemented by a fleet of airborne radars that can monitor airspace and coordinate friendly forces to respond. Indonesia has no comparable capabilities. Australia is also more proficient at operating long-range maritime patrol aircraft, of which Indonesia has few, and Australia has more modern and capable maritime strike capabilities.

Since the Falklands War, we have witnessed the growing vulnerability of big ships and seen that a defensive maritime strategy can work. The lesson has been amply reinforced in the Ukraine conflict. Tellingly, Ukraine scuttled its only major surface ship on the opening day of the war, fearing it would be sunk or captured by Russian forces. Ukraine has now taken the upper hand in the naval war despite not having a navy of its own. It has sunk the flagship of Russia's Black Sea Fleet and destroyed Russian ships and submarines in harbour in occupied Crimea. All were hit by missiles and drones launched either from land or from land-based aircraft.

The lesson here is not that Australia and Indonesia can do without navies. Rather, Ukraine is demonstrating that smaller countries can nullify the maritime power of much larger adversaries. And such a maritime strategy is not just militarily effective but politically reassuring because of its defensive character – it is designed solely to stop an adversary from using the oceans to project power onto land, but does not itself aim to project power. That will make it easier for Indonesia to embrace, and for it to be accepted in the region.

To reinforce this defensive character, the alliance needs one other element: an explicit commitment never to strike the territory of a foreign nation. This would make the military task of the alliance harder but diplomatically it is essential. There are signs that China has ambitions to develop military bases around the region. Evidence that China is developing a naval facility at Ream, Cambodia, is accumulating. We have also seen credible reports that China has approached Papua New Guinea and Vanuatu with proposals to host Chinese military facilities. These are worrying indicators, because foreign bases are essential for sustaining maritime operations far from home. China has accumulated truly impressive naval forces over the last two decades, but that fleet will always be hampered by South-East Asia's vast distances. It is difficult to concentrate maritime power over long distances and extended time periods if your force needs to make regular transits home to refuel, rearm, perform maintenance and rest. Foreign military bases alleviate that problem.

A naval base is a large, fixed target and therefore much easier to strike than individual ships at sea. It is also a more tempting target because it supports an entire fleet and, if destroyed, could turn a maritime campaign. So pledging not to hit such bases is a significant self-imposed constraint. Yet any suggestion that Indonesia and Australia would jointly attempt to neutralise such bases on the territory of third parties, especially fellow members of ASEAN, is a non-starter for both countries and for the region. The alliance should restrict itself to operating and attacking targets in the Indonesian and Australian maritime approaches.

To better understand the objective of this alliance, it is helpful to consider the most urgent practical case, which is Indonesia's dispute with China over who can claim the North Natuna Sea. China says Indonesia's North Natuna Sea exclusive economic zone slightly overlaps with its widely disputed "nine-dash line" claim. Indonesia is increasingly alarmed by China's growing assertiveness there. In 2021 a Chinese survey vessel loitered for a month around an Indonesian drilling rig in the North Natuna Sea. While Indonesia's armed and constabulary forces remain poorly trained and equipped to deal with such provocations, it has stepped up its efforts to protect its claims.

Australia and Indonesia … need a strategy focused on maritime denial

The critical question is whether Australia, if it was allied with Jakarta, could be drawn in to such a dispute.

Not exactly. The arrangement being proposed here is a last resort for both parties if they are being threatened from the sea by a hostile power. That doesn't mean such an alliance would be irrelevant to Indonesia's boundary dispute with China; in fact, the whole point of the arrangement is to guard against China achieving control over these maritime areas. However, it won't do this through joint Australian–Indonesian maritime policing of disputed seas. The proposal made here would not directly entangle Australia in these disputes. Rather, an alliance would set an upper limit to how far such disputes can escalate.

At present, in its disputes with South-East Asian countries over various islands and stretches of sea, China enjoys what strategists call "escalation dominance" – meaning the ability to maintain a superior position over the adversary, no matter the intensity or scale of the dispute. So when an unarmed Chinese survey vessel harasses an Indonesian oil rig, Indonesia could bring constabulary and naval vessels to the scene that would overwhelm the survey ship's meagre capabilities. But it's not the survey vessel Indonesia is worried about. Rather, Indonesia is thinking about what happens after it confronts that vessel. China has the largest coastguard fleet in the world, and the world's second-most powerful navy. Whatever Indonesia can bring to such a dispute, China can bring more. China has escalation dominance, which makes Indonesia reluctant to resist even if the initial balance of forces is favourable to it.

The purpose of this alliance would be to set an upper limit on escalation dominance, a point where, if China escalated a dispute to threats of military force against Indonesian territory, its dominance would evaporate. This does not mean Indonesia and Australia need to build vastly superior forces to those of China. The strategy advocated here is designed expressly to avoid arms racing by focusing exclusively on nullifying China's ability to project power. Australia and Indonesia won't need costly fleets. What they need is a strategy focused on maritime denial, as well as plentiful supplies of anti-ship weapons and the systems which support them, all designed simply to make China believe that if it uses its new navy to intimidate either country, the costs will outweigh the benefits. China will still be much stronger, but modern naval warfare overwhelmingly favours the defensive side over the one attempting to project force. Together, Indonesia and Australia can exploit this imbalance.

Risks

Despite its defensive character, an alliance like this would give Indonesia more confidence to defend its claims in the North Natuna Sea because it would know it has a backstop. It might no longer be so reticent to confront low-level Chinese harassment, and more willing to take risks. Of course, strengthening Indonesia's hand and weakening China's position in the South China Sea is precisely the goal. The point is to reduce the risk of Chinese dominance in maritime South-East Asia. Nevertheless, the alliance would tie Australia to potentially unpredictable Indonesian behaviour. A future Indonesian president may act erratically and commit Australia to a war that Jakarta provokes.

This risk is inherent in any alliance. Allies are dependent on each other for defence but are also at each other's mercy – when one country chooses to ally with another, they swap a fear of abandonment for one of entrapment. Even when one alliance partner acts recklessly, the others remain obligated to help them. On the other hand, the alliance might constrain Indonesia rather than embolden it, because Jakarta will understand the limits of what Australia will tolerate and will be unwilling to test those limits.

Still, entrapment is a risk. The real question is whether that risk outweighs the benefits. To make that judgement, Australia must persuade itself that Indonesia's security is important enough for Australia to justify some day fighting alongside Indonesia in a naval war against China. That's a stark and unfamiliar proposition – we rarely think about Indonesian security this way. But consider the commitments we seem ready to make to guard against threats that are far more distant. In our national debate, Taiwan's security has come to be seamlessly conflated with our own. When he was defence minister in 2021, the now Opposition leader, Peter Dutton, said it was "inconceivable" that Australia would not support the US in defending Taiwan if it were attacked by China. It's hard to imagine any senior minister saying something similar about coming to the aid of Indonesia. Yet Darwin is around 4300 kilometres away from Taipei, whereas Darwin to Jakarta is half that distance. It's a measure of how skewed our security debate has become that nobody questions the assumption that Taiwan's security is more important to Australia than Indonesia's security.

Form

Having examined what such an alliance would do, let's briefly consider what it would look like. First, the word "alliance" would almost certainly need to be banished because of Indonesia's long tradition of non-alignment. But the formal terms of such an agreement are less important than they might seem.

Indonesia has a substantial record of working with Australia on ambitious and far-reaching initiatives, even if they have stopped short of an alliance. The 1995 Suharto–Keating treaty, abrogated by Jakarta during the Timor crisis, didn't formally commit the parties to come to each other's defence, but Prime Minister Paul Keating described it as having "at least as much Realpolitik and clout as the Treaty we have with the United States", and saw it as an effort to complicate China's future planning, should it develop ambitions in South-East Asia. In 2006, a successor agreement known as the Lombok Treaty was signed, and several defence cooperation agreements have now been built on its foundations, with the latest one under negotiation.

Beijing's ambitions are bound to clash ever more directly with Indonesia's interests

When we think of the gold standard of international security treaties, we typically think of NATO, which formally commits its members to one another's defence. Yet a legal injunction means little in the absence of vital interests holding treaty members together. NATO is a credible alliance not because of the letter of the treaty but because its European members share a continent, so a threat against one is clearly a threat against all. It is the knowledge that all the parties have an obvious interest in working together that ultimately deters NATO's adversary.

Since an Australia–Indonesia alliance would probably not include a NATO-like statement of mutual defence, the parties would need to find other ways to communicate their willingness to come to each other's aid in the event of a security crisis. That could be done through joint military planning, joint training and doctrine, regular high-level meetings, and the basing of military forces on each other's territory. But the most important factor is for the two sides to jointly declare that they regard their part of the world as a shared strategic space in which the security of one from external threats is indivisible from that of the other.

What about the United States?

There is nothing in an Australia–Indonesia military alliance that threatens US interests or the US–Australia relationship. There is also plenty of historical evidence that Jakarta does not regard the US–Australia partnership as a barrier to closer relations with Canberra. So this proposal should in no way threaten the ANZUS alliance. Yet as Indonesian security analyst Evan Laksmana wrote in response to the September 2021 AUKUS announcement, "The more Australia weds itself strategically to the United States, the more entrenched its strategic divergence with Indonesia could be." ANZUS may be no barrier to an Australia–Indonesia alliance, but AUKUS certainly is.

The centrepiece of AUKUS is an agreement to supply the Royal Australian Navy with eight nuclear-powered submarines (SSNs). Less prominent but more significant (at least until the early 2040s, when Australia is scheduled to get its fourth SSN and thus achieve minimal operational capability) are two agreements announced after AUKUS to station US forces on Australian soil: the first is to upgrade the Northern Territory air base RAAF Tindal so that it can host American long-range bombers, while the second is for the HMAS Stirling naval base in Western Australia to be upgraded so that it can host a rotation of American nuclear-powered submarines. Both the AUKUS submarine deal and the basing announcements were made with China in mind. RAAF Tindal and HMAS Stirling will be equipped to allow American forces to stage combat missions against China. And the submarines Australia is buying have long range and endurance, making them perfectly suited to operating off China's coast to prevent the PLA Navy from breaking out into the open ocean. Australian SSNs could also be used to fire cruise missiles onto the Chinese landmass. As I argued in *Target Australia* (Australian Foreign Affairs 18, July 2023), those kinds of weapons and missions will make Australia a military target for China.

The effect on Indonesia's security, and on its willingness to ally with Australia, is material. South-East Asian countries including Indonesia have long expressed concern that their region could become a stage for US–China rivalry. Australia's actions make such worries more concrete: they give China's military an incentive to operate in and through the Indonesian archipelago rather than wait for US and Australian forces to get closer to China. Australia has traditionally thought of the Indonesian archipelago as a kind of moat protecting our continent. China now has the strongest possible incentive to operate nearer to us. We are inviting China, daring it, to cross the moat.

The AUKUS submarines and new US facilities in Australia will force Indonesia into some uncomfortable choices. If China does turn the Indonesian archipelago into a naval battleground, should

Indonesia remain neutral? Should it allow the US to use its airspace to fly from RAAF Tindal to its targets in China? Should it allow China to send missiles or bombers through its airspace to attack Tindal?

There are countless reasons for Australia to cancel the AUKUS submarine project; its impact on our relationship with Jakarta is just one. But if we must have nuclear-powered submarines, then at the very least, future Australian governments should repudiate the "impactful projection" rhetoric favoured by the present government and the attendant long-range strike capabilities being procured, including the purchase of cruise missiles that can hit the Chinese mainland. By word and deed, the government should communicate to Indonesia and the rest of South-East Asia that the Australian Defence Force, including its nuclear-powered submarine fleet, is designed to defend Australia and our maritime approaches, and not to pose a threat to China's territory and near seas. To reinforce that message, we should also step back from the US basing arrangements at HMAS Stirling and RAAF Tindal. This may be a tough sell in Washington, but we had a strong alliance with America before these announcements and it can withstand their cancellation.

Is it realistic?

There's no point proposing bold policy initiatives if the practical barriers to implementing them are insurmountable. It's possible to be persuaded by the logic of the argument made here while still dismissing it on pragmatic grounds – a military alliance between Jakarta and Canberra is so far from our present political reality, and faces so many barriers, that Australia would be wasting its time, resources and credibility pursuing it. Sure, Indonesia is open to ambitious security agreements, but this is a step beyond the Lombok Treaty. Why would Indonesia do it?

Let's not underestimate what Jakarta would be getting: not just a capable partner but a highly reliable one. As Indonesia grows wealthier and stronger, Australia will know that being Indonesia's partner is far preferable to having Jakarta view it with indifference or, worst of all, hostility. Indonesia is also getting further reassurance that it will never be threatened by Australia.

Yet Indonesia doesn't see China in the same way Australia does, and the fear in Jakarta would be that agreeing to a military alliance with Australia will pitch Indonesia towards a more confrontational position than it has ever been prepared to take. Indonesia also puts ASEAN at the core of its foreign policy and insists on maintaining non-alignment with the major powers. An agreement like this would be a big break from that pose. You can't be ASEAN-central if you are putting a lot of resources towards a non-ASEAN security initiative, and you can't be non-aligned if you sign a military treaty with an American ally.

These are reasonable points, and the plausibility of an Australia–Indonesia alliance rests on the expectation that Indonesia will become more open to such an agreement as its relationship with China deteriorates. Beijing's ambitions are bound to clash ever more directly with Indonesia's interests. Indonesia's continued commitment to Cold

War–era non-alignment has only been possible because no force was capable of pressuring Jakarta to move beyond it. China may be that force. Non-alignment is simply not relevant to the world Indonesia is entering, and ASEAN provides little resistance to China's ambitions. So Jakarta will have to take an increasingly assertive stance to defy China. The argument made here is simply that Indonesia can do this more effectively with Australia than without us.

Of course, Australia too will have to change. It will have to put aside concerns about allying with an illiberal country whose democracy is still fragile and might regress. Indonesia is also a nation with a bloody history of internal repression. We can be partly reassured by the fact that this agreement will focus exclusively on maritime security, which means dealing with Indonesia's navy and air force, not its army, the institution most implicated in past atrocities. But, more to the point, we will need to remind ourselves that the ultimate purpose of this alliance is to maintain the security of Indonesia and Australia against the unprecedented threat of Chinese domination. Politics is about choosing the lesser evil, and the point of this agreement is not to excuse or launder the reputation of a highly imperfect and often rancorous neighbour, but to prevent something disastrous from happening to both countries.

Finally, Australia will need to correct the violent course change it made in September 2021 when it announced AUKUS, and shortly thereafter the agreement to station US bombers and submarines on Australian soil. This requires, above all, a change of mindset about the region we live in and America's role in securing it. Although AUKUS was conceived by a centre-right government led by a conservative prime minister, Scott Morrison, this was reactionary policy, not conservative policy. America's status as the uncontested strategic leader of our region is evaporating, and by attempting to tie America down to the region through arms purchases and basing, Australia was trying to restore America's place in the regional security hierarchy. It was an attempt at a counter-revolution.

But we can't want a restoration of American power more than America itself wants it. The case for an alliance with Jakarta is built on unsentimental ground: Indonesia shares our geography and has just as much to lose as we do from a region dominated by China. The United States is not in that position, yet Australia is asking Washington to make enormous sacrifices on our behalf. We're betting on the US feeling compelled to fight China in our neighbourhood when it has no urgent need to do so. To have doubts about American commitment is not to make a moral judgement about its character or courage, but a prudential judgement about its interests. And if you wish to argue that alliances are built not just on the dispassionate calculation of interests but on common political traditions and decades of shared wartime sacrifice, then consider that Indonesia, too, has claims on our history and values.

But above all, remember that an alliance with Indonesia will signal not a break with Australian political tradition but the next step in the long evolution of Australian nationhood from Anglo-Saxon outpost to a multicultural nation deeply embedded in the economy, security and culture of our neighbourhood. ■

THE VIEW FROM JAKARTA

Friends with benefits, not fellow fighters

Evan A. Laksmana

As geopolitical uncertainties hang over the Indo-Pacific, can Australia rely on Indonesia as a close defence partner in a regional contingency? This question presumes, implicitly or otherwise, that the "enemy" in such a scenario would be China, and that the US alliance would underpin any war effort involving Australia. Despite the rhetoric around a regional balance of power or strategic equilibrium, what Australia ultimately seeks is to deter a regional conflict against China – and to prevail, should deterrence fail, with the help of the United States and its allies. According to the recently released National Defence Strategy, Australia specifically seeks a strategy of denial to change a potential adversary's belief that it could achieve its ambitions with military force.

Indonesia could be a key variable in this equation; the document after all calls the country Australia's "essential and enduring partner".

For one thing, Indonesia too should see China as a menacing threat. China's aggressive behaviour in recent years, challenging Indonesia's sovereign rights within its exclusive economic zones, from fisheries to hydrocarbon resources, as well its coercive economic, diplomatic and security tactics against Vietnam, Malaysia and the Philippines, exacerbates Jakarta's deteriorating security environment. When we consider that China has also fractured the cohesion and centrality of the Association of Southeast Asian Nations (ASEAN), which Jakarta dubs "the cornerstone" of its foreign policy, over the South China Sea, Indonesia should want to push back.

And Indonesia clearly has the potential to do so. As Sam Roggeveen argues in his book *The Echidna Strategy*, Indonesia's economy is big enough to withstand Chinese coercion and support a modern force with maritime capabilities. That China has had a shaky, if not acrimonious, standing in Indonesian political and domestic history – diplomatic ties were only reopened in the 1990s – makes it less likely that Jakarta would submit as a tributary state to China. It is therefore vital for Australia, Roggeveen argues, that Indonesia "becomes a counterweight to China".

Such expectations of Indonesia, however, misread the growing defence ties between Indonesia and Australia, and misjudge Indonesia's thinking around China and its regional environment. Indonesia ultimately sees Australia as a valuable provider of a specific set of defence needs – from education and training to combined exercises critical for readiness – and as a joint partner for a limited number of shared security challenges, such as illegal fishing or counterterrorism. Indonesia is unlikely ever to see Australia – or any other country, for that matter – as a future fellow war-fighter against China.

Indonesia arguably sees China as a strategic challenge, even if the defence, foreign policy, political and business communities cannot always reach a consensus on how to manage that challenge. Indonesia also finds China's expanding economic footprint in the country increasingly problematic: concerns over local political tensions, environmental protection and safety standards have been raised around major energy projects involving Chinese companies. However, Jakarta policymakers still consider it feasible to fundamentally hedge between – and to some extent compartmentalise – a China-tied economic prosperity and a Western-anchored security partnership. So long as Jakarta struggles to coherently deal with China as a strategic challenge, it is unlikely to seriously develop military options, including joining alliances with Australia or anyone else, against China.

Finally, Indonesia does not see the United States in the same way Australia does. While Canberra is seeking to double down on its alliance with Washington – AUKUS being the prime example of this – Jakarta does not define an increased US military presence as necessarily benign or reliable for its own security. Indeed, the likelihood of a US–China conflict has led to a resurgent discussion among defence policymakers and analysts about Indonesia developing its own "anti-access and area-denial" strategy against both China and the United States to ensure the neutrality of its waterways and airspace during wartime.

A friend in need

It often goes without saying, but it would take an existential threat for Indonesia to abandon its non-alignment foreign-policy principles. To be clear, non-alignment should not be simply about "neutrality" or a passive avoidance of tough choices. Non-alignment is instead a matter of finding well-calibrated terms of engagement with different strategic partners to defend particular sets of interests. Perhaps the only "red line" in this regard is a military alliance, and no Indonesian government since the 1950s has been willing to pay the domestic costs of crossing that.

Short of that, Jakarta has been open to participating in a wide range of foreign-policy mechanisms which might address its security concerns – from ASEAN to bilateral strategic partnerships and minilateral arrangements like the Malacca Straits Patrol, which also involves Malaysia, Singapore and Thailand. Common features of these are the ability for Jakarta to feel it is an equal partner – if not a veto player – in the process; the fact that their outcomes ultimately lead to a more strategic manoeuvring space; and that Indonesia's domestic political and economic needs are also addressed.

Within these broad contours of Indonesian foreign policy, Australia is not necessarily the highest priority. Indonesia's economic prosperity, as far as its elites are concerned, is not tied deeply to Australia, although new avenues such as the green transition, the digital economy and energy security could change that. The Comprehensive Economic Partnership Agreement (CEPA) between the two countries only came into force in 2020. Indonesia and Australia are each other's thirteenth-most important trading partner. Indonesia ranks twenty-seventh as an Australian foreign investment destination, and is the thirty-eighth-largest investor in Australia.

Indonesia's security interests are also not wedded to or dependent on Australia alone. Canberra and Jakarta's shared security challenges, whether they concern internal security matters, like Papua, or transnational issues such as illegal fishing or counterterrorism, are not existential. If anything, the fact that internal military documents note Australia's importance for Indonesia's military diplomacy is likely shaped by concerns around Papua and the lingering memories of East Timorese independence. While Australia does not threaten Indonesia's security, it also does not make its protection necessarily better or more effective. It is unlikely, for example, that Australia alone can help reduce Indonesia's maritime security risks and vulnerabilities in its archipelagic sea lanes or the South China Sea.

The fact that Indonesia's domestic political elites and strategic policymakers do not react with hostility to Australia's growing economic, social or political presence and engagement – and we cannot say the same of China's – is a good indication of the potential to grow the bilateral relationship. After all, a large group of Indonesians from all walks of life, including defence policymakers, have visited and studied at various Australian educational institutions. The lack of strong reactions, however, could also indicate Australia's marginal status for Indonesian policymakers.

Regardless, the reverse case cannot easily be made. Australia needs security from Indonesia more than Indonesia needs it from Australia. Australia's geographic position – and its cultural "fear of abandonment", as Allan Gyngell called it – requires it to have strong allies to fend off potential threats from or through Indonesia. Successive Australian defence policymakers and documents have expressed variations on this theme since the Cold War.

In a future US–China conflict, for example, Indonesia's geography makes it strategically crucial for any military and economic movements to or from the north. Alternatively, if Indonesia were to become hostile towards Australia, especially after reaching its economic and military potential, the latter's security would be in question. The broader point is simply that Indonesia matters more to Australia than the other way around.

Indonesia is unlikely to consider Australia as one of the "cornerstones" of its foreign policy – that status has largely been reserved for ASEAN. China and the United States also matter more, for historical as well as economic and security reasons. Other regional powers, such as Japan, as well as key neighbours like Singapore and Malaysia, are also higher priorities, given their economic, political, defence and social ties to Indonesia. Australia could one day share similar status but is unlikely to exceed these countries in terms of their importance for Indonesia.

Still, both Jakarta and Canberra have been committed to elevating their relationship for almost two decades now. Following the 2006 Lombok Treaty, relations have improved significantly. Canberra is among the top investors in ASEAN mechanisms and has sought closer foreign-policy coordination, if not alignment, with Jakarta on a range of issues. The CEPA underpins a growing set of economic and people-to-people ties, along with education and defence partnerships. Arguably, despite the occasional hiccups, Indonesia–Australia relations today are better than ever before.

The challenge ahead, however, is not about managing the bilateral relationship alone, though much work remains to be done. But the foundation for that effort is in place; defence ties could even be further elevated soon under a new deal (being discussed at the time of writing). The challenge instead lies in the broader questions surrounding the regional order, given that Indonesia and Australia arguably hold divergent strategic views on the matter. Today, their divergences are perhaps overlaid by bilateral priorities and engagements. But the polarising pressures of the US–China strategic competition and the prospect of a regional conflict could sharpen those differences between Jakarta and Canberra.

Differences over the United States and China

The primary divergence revolves around the military role of the US in the region. Indonesia is unlikely to view the US as a benevolent provider of regional security, as Australia does. Indonesia's troubled past with the United States – and its geostrategic vulnerability of being strategically located between the Indian and Pacific oceans without the capabilities to fully secure its strategic waterways and airspace – means that

Jakarta will from time to time view the US as a possible interventionist great power. The fact that its domestic political and economic system is not resilient to external pressures exacerbates those tendencies. Some senior policymakers still recite how the US kicked Indonesia while it was down during the Asian financial crisis, or how the disastrous Iraq War and the non-ratification of the United Nations Convention on the Law of the Sea (UNCLOS) undermined the international rules-based order. The recent war in Gaza has exacerbated this credibility perception in Jakarta.

Defence policymakers privately also cited instances in which the United States was seen as intruding into Indonesian airspace in the early 2000s as one of the rationales for Indonesian defence modernisation. The prospect in 2019 of the US sanctioning Indonesia under the *Countering America's Adversaries Through Sanctions Act* (CAATSA) as the country was finalising its purchase of Russian arms brought back the bitter experience of the US military embargo in the 1990s and 2000s. Cold War memories of US support for regional rebels in the 1950s have not entirely faded either.

Despite this history, Indonesia–US defence ties remain strong. In the past two decades, more than 7300 Indonesian students have trained in some 200 US military education and training programs. Indonesia has held more than 100 major military exercises with the United States and imported close to US$1 billion in arms and equipment during the same period. Under defence minister Prabowo Subianto – now the president-elect – Indonesia has sought to acquire more advanced weaponry and equipment from the West.

These trends notwithstanding, Jakarta does not always see the American military presence as a net positive, nor will it accept that its security can only be guaranteed by it. And yet Australia is doubling down on its alliance. While that step, which includes long-term programs like AUKUS, is perhaps a reasonable strategic bet for Canberra, Indonesia cannot be entirely faulted for thinking that the "deputy sheriff" myth is alive and kicking. The more closely Australia ties itself to the United States, the more entrenched its divergence with Indonesia could be.

Australia therefore risks being caught not only between the US and China but between Jakarta and Washington too. While Indonesia sees Australia as a valuable defence partner as it seeks to meet a specific set of security needs, it isn't going to join a US-led coalition in a war against China. The hope that Australia can have its cake and eat it too – deepening its military alliance with the US, growing its defence ties with Indonesia, boosting ASEAN centrality and benefiting from China's economic growth while containing its military assertiveness – seems increasingly untenable. Hope, after all, is not strategy.

Indonesia, meanwhile, is unlikely to see China the way Australia does. China certainly presents a strategic challenge. But given Indonesia's own bloody anti-communist past, bilateral historical acrimony with China, domestic political sensitivities and elite-led economic interdependence, there isn't going to be a consensus that China is an existential threat in a way that would require Jakarta to join an anti-China military coalition.

That some Western policymakers, including in Canberra, still cling to the notion that all it will take for Indonesia to join a counterbalancing coalition against China is a demonstration of China's aggressive intent and behaviour is yet another example of uninformed aspirations. Indonesia is indeed worried about how the US–China competition has been polarising the region. It is the nature of the interaction between the two powers, not which is the universally better or the most belligerent of the two, that matters for Jakarta.

At one level, this speaks to the pressure on Jakarta from competing domains – from defence, economics, trade, technology and education – that shrinks Indonesia's options. Jakarta, like many of its regional counterparts, perhaps still clings to the idea of strategic compartmentalisation – cooperation over different issues with different partners. This aspiration becomes harder to sustain as both Washington and Beijing seek to grow their own exclusionary networks across multiple policy areas. Being part of a technological or defence or economic network with one great power could exclude a country from another set of networks by another great power.

But Jakarta is also concerned about the likelihood of regional flashpoints turning into all-out conflict between China and the United States and its allies. These flashpoints have led to more frequent and enduring crises across the Indo-Pacific as the great-power competition turns "operational encounters" into "strategic problems". We see this across the region, from the India–China border and Myanmar to the South China Sea, the Taiwan Strait and the Korean Peninsula and beyond.

The concern for Indonesia is not just whether "one side" is behind the provocation or aggression, but whether a regional conflict becomes more likely as tensions rise. In other words, Indonesia is concerned with the competitive interactions between the US and China that shape a wide range of regional relationships. For Indonesia, the onus to prevent a wider regional conflict is on both the United States and China. This worldview underpins the growing debate in Jakarta over the need for the country to develop its own version of "anti-access and area-denial" thinking and capabilities.

All-round anti-access

The principle of anti-access – which is about deterring or challenging a superior force from using or entering key areas that you hope to control – has been part of Indonesia's doctrinal precepts since the 1960s.

Indonesia's Total People's Defence doctrine, developed in the 1950s and 1960s (and still in place in different iterations), has always assumed that its future enemy will be militarily superior and will seek to control access into and over its strategic geography. Its "layered defence" strategy assumes the need to deny access to the country's interior lines of operation by defending the "buffer zone" beyond the 200-nautical-mile exclusive economic zone. The capability to wage guerrilla warfare acts as an ultimate deterrence, should this strategy fail.

In a war in which it is not directly involved as a belligerent, Indonesia's concern would be to preserve the "military neutrality" of its strategic waterways and airspace. Some of these routes fall under what are known as "archipelagic sea lanes" cutting across from the Pacific to the Indian Oceans – essentially between Australia and the first and second island chains. While under UNCLOS Indonesia needs to keep its designated sea lanes open, a wartime condition where, for example, opposing belligerents "fight it out" in or through those waterways would likely be a key concern.

Leaving aside debates about legality, defence policymakers and analysts have examined what sort of military capabilities would be required for Indonesia to "enforce" the neutrality of its waterways. Andi Widjajanto, governor of Indonesia's National Resilience Institute until late 2023, developed a set of "anti-access protocols" that the country needs to develop, ranging from air–sea patrols to maritime denial and cyber defence. Senior members of the Indonesian Air Force have also debated the need to have an "air shield" strategy to prevent unwarranted access to the country's airspace. The defence ministry issued several regulations in 2023 that codified some of this emerging anti-access thinking into future defence planning.

Beyond the feasibility of these policies, the broader point is that Indonesia's defence and foreign-policy establishment is concerned about wartime access to its waterways and airspace. The concern is not directed against one party only: it applies to China as much as to the United States and its allies, including Australia. Indonesia, after all, cannot afford to be "selectively" anti-access, as this would position it as a belligerent. Joining Australia in an anti-China coalition is an example of such a scenario.

The final challenge is whether and how Indonesia can secure access to the resources located within its exclusive maritime zones during peacetime. The problem here is less about strategic waterways access or neutrality and more about maritime law enforcement. The task for Jakarta is not just about pushing back against illegal incursions – by China but also Vietnam, Malaysia and others – into Indonesian exclusive economic zones. It is also about fundamentally transforming the country's maritime security policy and boosting diplomatic efforts, whether bilaterally or multilaterally, to manage maritime security challenges with regional partners.

The challenge by China, in other words, in and around Indonesia's exclusive economic zone in the North Natuna Sea has not been perceived by Jakarta as an existential threat. Short of direct occupation of one of the Natuna islands, Indonesia will tend to view the incursions as a challenge for maritime law enforcement, regional diplomacy and international law. If anything, Indonesian policymakers fear that militarising their response to China's behaviour could allow Beijing to "play the victim" and internationalise the issue further – or might even inadvertently acknowledge China's illegal claims in the area by being forced into any kind of negotiations or agreements over "maritime rights".

The challenges that China poses to Indonesia, which for Australian policymakers should position the country as a natural ally, are viewed differently by Jakarta. If anything, the anti-access thinking, when applied to wartime, envisions a future conflict in which both the

US and China are held equally responsible, and both should therefore be deterred away from Indonesia's strategic waterways and airspace. In peacetime, China's incursion has yet to be viewed as an existential threat. The notion that Australia and Indonesia could work together to counterbalance China seems unwarranted at this point. Indonesia does not prefer a regional order under a *pax Sinica* – but that does not translate into a preference for a *pax Americana*.

Neither friend nor foe

Indonesia–Australia defence ties today are perhaps at their strongest in more than a decade. Despite occasional hiccups, the post–Lombok Treaty dynamic has gone from strength to strength, with personnel exchanges, major exercises and arms transfers. The risk is that Australia wrongly interprets these strong defence ties as meaning that its strategic outlook will converge with Indonesia's, or that Jakarta will be a reliable defence partner against China.

Indonesia needs engagement and defence cooperation programs with Australia to improve its own readiness and professionalism, especially given its under-resourced educational, exercise and training infrastructure. Indeed, the defence ties between the two nations rest heavily on education and training exchanges as well as joint exercises, rather than arms sales or technological collaboration, let alone joint war-fighting or shared operational history. Indonesia, in other words, prefers a friend with benefits, not a fellow war-fighter in an exclusive alliance.

Furthermore, the ties have not been tested in a serious contingency since 1999, during the East Timor situation. In the event of a future regional war – say, over Taiwan – does Australia expect Indonesia to do nothing, or even to facilitate the passage of Australia's assets, including nuclear-powered subs, through Indonesian waters on their way to the first island chain? What if China seeks to prevent that? If Papua becomes another East Timor–style fiasco, will Australia be ready to do nothing and to support Indonesia no matter what? These questions should give us pause as we consider whether Indonesia and Australia might work together militarily.

In a Prabowo presidency, set to begin in October 2024, the strategic divergence between Australia and Indonesia over the role of the US and China is unlikely to narrow. For one thing, the president-elect has repeatedly said that he will continue President Joko Widodo's policies, including on the growing economic and financial ties with China. That Prabowo's first foreign visit as president-elect in April 2024 was to Beijing perhaps also signals China's nervousness about him. Will he return to his previous hostile rhetoric on China and ethnic-Chinese Indonesians, which goes back to the 1990s? Or will he be closer to Widodo's policies of opening the door as wide as possible for China's growing economic engagement with Indonesia?

These questions notwithstanding, Prabowo's tenure as defence minister since 2019 has been distinguished by his courting of American and Western powers to support his procurement policies. By some estimates, Prabowo signed defence procurement contracts potentially worth more than US$20 billion during his tenure, the majority of which went to American and European companies. His frequent overseas visits as defence minister have also mostly centred on these countries. He has boosted Indonesia's broader defence partnerships with a range of countries, including Australia, and has been more "understanding" of initiatives such as AUKUS than other members of the Indonesian foreign policy establishment.

But what we are likely to see ahead is not an Indonesian presidency that leans closer to the West but one that will hedge even harder. Prabowo's victory cannot be detached from the country's major business groups – many of whom have strong ties to Chinese companies – as well as from Widodo's policies and key personnel. Prabowo's administration will seek to soothe concerns in Beijing and expand China's economic presence in Indonesia. But he will also ensure that his defence procurement deals move forward. He is likely, in other words, to oversee more strategic compartmentalisation, whereby Indonesia's economic ties with China and security ties with the West grow in parallel.

Indonesia therefore will remain squarely in the middle of the hedging pack, perhaps alongside countries like Vietnam, between the US and China. It will remain sceptical of both great powers, while still seeking to benefit in different ways from each. Attempts to modernise the Indonesian National Defence Force (TNI) will continue, even if procurement alone is unlikely to solve its plethora of doctrinal and organisational challenges. Defence partnerships with countries such as Australia are likely to expand, even if a broader strategic alignment remains elusive. China's behaviour across the region will continue to pose uneasy questions for Jakarta's foreign-policy makers – but it will not be so critically difficult that they must develop serious military options about it, let alone forge an alliance with Australia.

To be clear, there is plenty of room for Indonesia and Australia to develop their defence and security partnership. The "soft" defence cooperation programs around education, training and exercises – and Australia is already Indonesia's top partner in this regard, after perhaps the US – could use some "harder" edge of defence technology research and development, as well as industrial collaboration. Shared security challenges at sea, whether in the Indian or Pacific oceans, could see more collaboration between the Indonesian and Australian navies and maritime security agencies. There are also a wide range of security challenges, from counterterrorism to illegal trafficking and climate change, where there is room to grow the Indonesia–Australia security partnership.

But a peacetime security partnership is unlikely to translate into a wartime collaboration, especially when China is the opponent. Abstract notions of a rules-based order will never entirely persuade Jakarta policymakers – well aware of the country's challenging history and contemporary problems – of the need to join forces with Australia against China. There are difficult conversations to be had between Jakarta and Canberra over more than just the state of their bilateral relations. The shape and future of the regional order – and how to get there – requires both nations to be realistic in their expectations and clear-eyed in their choices. ■

THE CHAMELEON

Will Prabowo be a strongman or a statesman?

Emma Connors

In the days that followed Prabowo Subianto's victory in Indonesia's presidential election on 14 February 2024, two revealing developments took place.

On 19 February, the Prabowo camp confirmed that it was unlikely the internationally respected finance minister Sri Mulyani would continue in her role from October, when the new administration is sworn in. This split between Prabowo and Sri Mulyani gives foreign investors circling the country pause for thought. During the election campaign, a long-simmering dispute between the two regarding defence spending – Sri Mulyani was against a big increase sought by Prabowo – had become public. Was this the reason for the split, or did Prabowo intend to block reform and fiscal discipline and fear Sri Mulyani would oppose him? Then, on 20 February, the OECD announced it had begun accession discussions with Indonesia. This was an important marker of the country's ascent from the wrecked state it was in a quarter of century ago, after the political, social and economic chaos triggered by the Asian Financial Crisis.

These two events epitomise the choices facing modern Indonesia, a beguiling, confusing and occasionally frustrating place where, as one long-term Jakarta resident summed it up, "almost everything is difficult and almost anything is possible".

The 2024 election result will be hugely consequential for Indonesia, South-East Asia's rising power. Will Prabowo follow the painstaking reform process that Mulyani has helped shepherd, including moves to counter the concentration of power that fans crony capitalism? Or will the country's new leader prove to be an anti-liberal economic ultranationalist?

On 20 March, Indonesia's General Election Commission released the final results of the vote, in which 164 million people – representing 82 per cent of those registered – made their choices for president and vice president. The Prabowo ticket had secured 59 per cent of votes, followed by Anies Baswedan with 25 per cent and Ganjar Pranowo with 16 per cent.

Prabowo's rivals, and others dismayed by the actions of the incumbent president, Joko "Jokowi" Widodo, leading up to the vote, have raised concerns about the weakening of democratic institutions in the country. In the days before the election, millions watched a documentary titled *Dirty Vote,* which alleged selective distribution of social assistance was among the measures used to boost the Prabowo ticket.

However, their substantial winning margin has enabled Prabowo and his running mate to stare down the allegations of voting fraud made by his opponents. On 22 April, Indonesia's Constitutional Court ruled that there was no evidence of systemic fraud, presidential interference or the swaying of votes by government handouts or any other action. Anies and Ganjar said they would respect the verdict.

So on inauguration day, 20 October 2024, Prabowo is set to be sworn in as Indonesia's president three days after his seventy-third birthday, and Gibran Rakabuming Raka, Jokowi's oldest son, will become vice president a few weeks after he turns thirty-seven. They make a fascinating combination. Prabowo, a serial presidential candidate, has waited decades to lead his country. Gibran suddenly appeared on the ticket just days before the nominations were finalised last year. The entrepreneur-turned-mayor had already departed from his avowed determination to avoid politics when his father became president a decade ago. Still, few believe his metamorphosis into vice presidential candidate was solely the product of his own ambition. Jokowi's dynastic yearnings, the country surmised, could no longer be denied. The manoeuvring to enable Gibran to contest the VP slot despite technically being too young fuelled concerns that Jokowi had his thumb on the scale.

The question, then, is how much influence the outgoing president will have on the new. The elites who flourished in the Jokowi era, and the millions of others who liked him and thought he did a good job, assume Prabowo will stick to his pledge to continue the course set by Jokowi. These include taking steps to open the country to foreign investment to help fund infrastructure and industrial development. After a decade in power, Jokowi's approval ratings still hover at around 80 per cent. His support helped secure victory for Prabowo, who could continue to bask in that reflected glory if he tones down some of his fiery nationalism and follows Jokowi's emphasis on economic diplomacy, where external relations are directed at Indonesia's progress to OECD-stamped developed country status. In this scenario, while the style might differ, the substance of what has been dubbed "Jokowinomics" will continue. And, of course, the former president will retain personal influence through his son, the vice president.

Others suggest it's unlikely the incoming leader will share any of the considerable power he will command once installed in the Presidential Palace. In the days following the election, there were two recurring topics of conversation in Jakarta: shock that Prabowo had secured such a large majority, and the certainty of uncertainty. The foreign investment community had been relaxed about the election outcome – for the first time, there was no rush to shift capital out of the country ahead of the vote. People assumed that whoever won would do as their predecessors had: install capable technocrats to run the machinery of government while giving a few plum roles to those who had helped pave their way to victory. Indonesia's slow march to prosperity would continue.

But Prabowo the presumptive president is different from Prabowo the candidate. Over the decades, the former military general, who speaks five languages, has reinvented himself several times. No one can be certain how his presidency will play out.

Prabowo and Australia

In the last five years, Prabowo has crisscrossed the globe in his role as defence minister, offering his views on topics as diverse as a rising China and Russia's war in Ukraine. In a visit to Beijing in April, Prabowo assured China's leader, Xi Jinping, that he "fully supported" the development of closer Indonesia–China relations. China's incursions into Indonesia's fishing zones in the South China Sea remain an irritant, but Indonesia is used to playing the long game with China. A few years ago, Prabowo urged all countries to respect China as a "great civilisation". China's ascent is one reason why global powers are increasingly inclined to notice Indonesia, the largest economy in South-East Asia. This is one of the world's fastest-growing regions, and a buffer between China and a United States determined to maintain sway in Asia. Indonesia is also a vital maritime power, with more than 45 per cent of seaborne trade passing through its waters.

Australia has always kept a nervous eye on its northern neighbour. The 2023 Lowy Institute Poll suggests that while most Australians trust Japan (85 per cent), the United Kingdom (84 per cent) and France (79 per cent) to act responsibly in the world, only 51 per cent feel the same way about Indonesia.

At an official level, the presumptive president has worked closely as defence minister with his Australian counterpart in recent years. The bilateral relationship tends to be stronger when Labor is in power in Canberra. Scrape away the formal diplomacy, though, and country-to-country links are thin. Last year Indonesia overtook New Zealand as the favourite short-stay destination for Australians, but few know much about the place beyond the holiday mecca of Bali. Cultural links are tenuous. Trade and investment links are relatively weak, reflecting the fact that these two resource-exporting nations have traditionally competed rather than complemented each other. Indonesia is the world's biggest exporter of coal, followed by Australia, and when a frosty bilateral relationship saw China stop buying coal from Australia, Indonesia stepped up. This aspect of the relationship also came into focus in 2024 after Indonesia's controversial nickel policies flooded the market and brought some Australian mines to a standstill.

On the plus side, there are signs that a free trade agreement signed four years ago is bearing fruit, particularly in services, where the two economies are better matched. Australia's expertise in health and education, for example, dovetails with Indonesia's need to maximise its demographic dividend.

It's reasonable to assume these links will strengthen over the next decade, given Indonesia's trajectory. It's tipped to reach top ten economy status in the next decade, and top five by 2040, up from its current pegging at around sixteenth. There's a renewed focus from Canberra on bolstering economic ties with the region, and Indonesia's push to become an electric-vehicle powerhouse sees a role for Australia's lithium – one reason for the new administration to continue to court Australia among bigger trading partners.

However, Prabowo is also an ultranationalist and a former military commander linked to state-sanctioned violence in Indonesia's authoritarian past. He has repeatedly expressed his distaste for economic neoliberalism, and has at times aligned himself with hardline Islam. In short, he embodies many of the facets of Indonesia that make Westerners uneasy at a time when it has never been as advantageous to Australia to engage closely with the country he will soon lead.

Uncomfortable as it may be, Prabowo's past makes it imperative that Australia looks to the future. With around half of the nation's 275 million people aged under thirty, you can be sure that's the direction Indonesia is focused on.

Capitalism with Indonesian characteristics

If you travel to a fishing village on one of Indonesia's far-flung islands, you might take a cursory look and conclude not much has changed since the mid-1990s, when Prabowo's then father-in-law Suharto still held the country tight in a totalitarian grip.

That would be a mistake. Like other developing countries, technology has allowed Indonesia to leapfrog several generations of communication. Many Indonesians remain unbanked but few lack a mobile phone. In fact, many people have more than one. The country is the third-largest mobile phone market globally (behind China and India) with 355 million active subscriptions.

Demand for digital services and entertainment appears to be insatiable. That's attracted the likes of America's Google and China's Alibaba. Home-grown tech giants have also flourished, including super-app developer GoTo and Bukalapak, the ecommerce platform with 100 million customers that has set up a base in Australia to help scout talent.

As always, there's an Indonesia-first element to regulation in the tech sector, with the Jokowi government recently banning social media companies from engaging in commerce because it figured local players were losing out. TikTok's Chinese parent, ByteDance, has fallen in line, agreeing to invest US$1.5 billion in a joint venture that has united GoTo's Tokopedia with TikTok Shop Indonesia.

This transaction is a neat example of how foreign investors follow the terms of play dictated by Indonesia's economic nationalism, which is rooted in Pancasila, the state philosophy formulated by the country's first prime minister, Sukarno. When you buy into Indonesia, you buy into its way of doing business, where nationalism overrules laissez-faire. Prabowo is a firm advocate for the founding principles, which promote a "middle path" between capitalism and socialism and emphasise egalitarianism and social justice.

While this emphasis on "communitarianism" has been a constant, Prabowo's winning election campaign – in which religion was not front and centre – represented a break from the past. In 2019 Prabowo forcefully played the religion card, aligning with hardline Muslims as religious moderates sided with Jokowi. The rival sides framed that presidential race as a contest between a communist takeover (through Jokowi) and a caliphate (which, it was argued, would be enabled by a Prabowo victory).

In 2024, moderate voices swung behind Prabowo for pragmatic reasons to do with funding and favours. Still, it's significant that religion was not a hot-button issue. Indonesia has not always been a glowing example of a pluralistic society, but this election could mark a turning point, suggests Sandiaga Uno, the politician who was Prabowo's running mate in 2019. Using the Arabic term, he cites "*wasathiyyah*", the Islamic value of moderation. He believes the "middle path" no longer faces serious political opposition in Indonesia because the majority support the Pancasila vision of "unity in diversity".

"When you mix Islam and politics you don't win here," Sandiaga said in an interview at his Jakarta home just a few days before the election. "You have to have an element of Islam in your key messages but clearly as a nation we believe in Pancasila. Maybe that is Jokowo's legacy – an end to this course of Islam versus nationalism."

On election night, Prabowo made tacit reference to this, declaring that he and Gibran would serve as the president and vice president for all Indonesian people, and would protect all citizens, "regardless of their ethnicity, religion, or social background". Peaceful coexistence is easier when people have jobs and believe their children will be adequately educated. Prabowo has promised to continue and extend the gains made under Jokowi by accelerating the economic expansion that generates jobs and helps fund schools, roads and hospitals.

In particular, he has pledged to continue Jokowi's downstreaming policies that have turbo-charged the development of massive industrial parks. International investors, led by China's steel giant Tsingshan Holding Group, have poured billions of dollars into the largest of these, which has transformed a small village in the Morowali Regency on the island of Sulawesi into 3000 hectares of mining, smelting and acid-based treatment of nickel ore.

These activities accelerated after Indonesia banned all exports of processed nickel in 2020. The ban was contested by the European Union, and the World Trade Organization found in its favour. Indonesia has appealed the decision. It will presumably come up in the OECD accession process, which prizes open trade and investment, though there is no timeline for these talks. Prabowo has vowed to double down and ban other resource exports, with the hope of expanding value-add industries.

During the election campaign, Prabowo told voters he would not adhere to neoliberalism. "The government is not merely the regulator; the government is the pioneer and, if needed, intervenes to work and help the people," he said. It's a popular view inside Indonesia. What's not known is whether Prabowo will follow Jokowi's lead in pushing through changes that help to insulate foreign investors from some of the excesses of economic nationalism. Jokowi also stood clear and let the finance ministry and central bank continue their two-decades-long journey to instil the fiscal and macroeconomic disciplines that have coaxed foreign capital back into the country.

This progress could have been derailed by the global health crisis that struck just as Australian and Indonesia concluded their free trade agreement. However, Indonesia emerged from the pandemic on a surer economic footing than many had dared hope. In the alarming early days of COVID-19, international advisers warned their clients that civil unrest on a massive scale was imminent. They warned that riots and violence would push Indonesia back into the late 1990s, a time when many expected the country would fall apart much as Yugoslavia had.

The pandemic was awful. Infection control was marred in the early days by mixed messages, and the official death toll of 160,941 doubtless understates the reality. But the Jokowi government embarked on a massive stimulus campaign to offset the loss of jobs and livelihoods, and markets barely blinked.

Since then, the Indonesian rupiah has survived a surging American dollar and global inflation. With a current account in good shape, foreign investment has poured in at record levels in recent years. Even Australian businesses, which have traditionally looked elsewhere for overseas expansion, are in the mix. The health and education sectors are opening up, offering Australia the chance to expand its exports beyond the traditional wheat, coal and livestock.

Doing business in Indonesia

Under Jokowi, Indonesia's particular mix of capitalism and socialism has increasingly made room for privately owned businesses to provide services to its growing middle class. This has brought opportunity for Australian companies, particularly in the service sectors, where the Australian brand is strong.

Later this year, for instance, Sydney-based Recce Pharmaceuticals expects to begin a late-stage trial of a synthetic anti-infective in Indonesia. Known as Recce 327, the intravenous and topical therapy is designed to treat serious and potentially life-threatening infections.

Recce is working with Indonesia's PT Etana Biotechnologies and the government research agency BRIN and drug regulator BPOM.

Health minister Budi Gunadi Sadikin – who has been floated as a possible finance minister by Prabowo – is among those supporting the partnership. If the Phase 3 trial is successful, the new therapy could be fast-tracked and in use in Indonesia within three months. It would be the first Australian-developed drug and one of the few non-generics – that is, a drug still under patent – to become widely available in Indonesia.

Recce CEO James Graham is thrilled at the reception his company has had. Unexpectedly, he says, this was a "pull initiative". "They approached us. And frankly, if they hadn't, it would have been a 'we'll be there one day maybe' scenario," he said.

Indonesia's health ministry sees several opportunities converging, said Roy Himawan, the ministry's director of pharmaceutical and medical device resilience. "As a developing country, we need to choose partners that will help develop our pharma manufacturing sector as our health spending continues to grow," he said. This goal has previously led to collaborations with Chinese and Indian firms. Now, with the Australian and Indonesian health ministries signing a memorandum of understanding a couple of years ago, that's extending to Australia.

For decades, wealthy Indonesians have left the country to get access to the latest drugs and treatments. The government estimates that almost two million engage in medical tourism each year, spending up to US$10 billion. Emerging countries have traditionally made do with older, off-patent medicines, prompting wealthier citizens to travel abroad to access the latest drugs. Singapore and Bangkok have long been the destinations of choice for Indonesians who can afford to travel for health.

For those who can't, a slow revolution is underway. This year marks a decade since the Indonesian government introduced a national health insurance scheme, which includes a register of approved medicines. The scheme now covers more than 80 per cent of the population and, according to one government study, has reduced out-of-pocket payments by 40 per cent. A medical emergency is now less likely to be a financial emergency, particularly for those in poor and rural communities – though this partly reflects a lack of supply of medical services in poorer areas of the country.

Indonesia still has a low ratio of hospital beds to population, lagging most of its neighbours in South-East Asia. In West Java, an Australian-based multinational, Aspen Medical, anchors a bold project aiming to build a string of international hospitals and hundreds of clinics. Dr Andrew Rochford, who leads the project, has been involved in healthcare in the country for more than a decade, since he realised he didn't have to go as far as India or Africa to take medical innovation to the developing world. He's now gone from being a medico to a cultural go-between.

"In most meetings we have with our partners here, my role is to make sure that by the end of the meeting both sides are on the same page," Rochford says. "Quite often, our team will go away and say, 'Oh that was great.' And I'll say, 'Yeah, they might have said that, but this is what they actually mean.' We're all trying to achieve the same things but for historical and cultural reasons there are subtle nuances that you need to know how to translate – and it's more than just language."

Nationalism is a potent, shaping force. "When I describe Indonesia to people, I emphasise it's a young country – it's only seventy years or so since independence – with a strong and endearing national pride," says Rochford.

Big leaps are possible – in healthcare, education and emerging green economy sectors – through partnerships, Rochford believes. He has faith that provincial and central governments are committed to making the necessary adjustments in regulation to bring foreign players in. "There is this real drive to meet the huge goal of making Indonesia the fourth-largest economy in the world."

In the tertiary education sector, Australia's Monash University is at the forefront of change, opening the first foreign-owned campus in Indonesia in October 2021. Others are following. Western Sydney University plans to enrol its first students in Surabaya, in East Java; Deakin University has joined with the United Kingdom's Lancaster to open a campus in Bandung, West Java; and Central Queensland University is looking beyond Java to Indonesia's territory on the island of Borneo.

Andrew MacIntyre, who took the Monash University Indonesia campus from idea to reality, said it has been a highlight of his career. Recently retired, he's among those trying to change the Australian mindset toward partnerships with our northern neighbour.

"We have to stop looking at investments in the country as a form of foreign aid," he argues. "In fact, the reverse is true. It's a privilege to be given the right to try and earn a place."

This is not to downplay the challenges involved – even if you have buy-in from the very top. "We had the backing of the president and the education minister, and that helps, but it's not enough – because their offices are not where the approvals are," MacIntyre points out. "Indonesia has a really complex regulatory framework. Many aspects contradict each other or are not clear. The further down we went, the harder it got. And it was never because people were stupid, corrupt, or lazy. Rather, the problem was almost always that one part of Indonesian regulation didn't agree with another. So we had to find ways of helping people to change things, and that required building political coalitions across the top of government."

Of course, it would be easier to do business in markets that are more familiar, like the United Kingdom, New Zealand, Europe or the United States. But that's not where the growth will be, at least as far as Australian universities are concerned.

"We have done very well with our education exports, but we are getting close to the peak when it comes to overseas students in Australia," says MacIntyre. "There's a lot more competition, particularly from Asia, where more and more universities are offering courses in English – so there's one of our big advantages gone. And the region's universities are getting better and better – that's what you get after thirty years of economic expansion."

Growth prospects

Educating Western markets about Indonesia is something Sri Mulyani knows all about. The respected economist was Indonesia's finance minister from 2005 till 2010. She then joined the World Bank as managing director, but returned to government in 2016 to again lead the Finance Ministry through Jokowi's second five-year term. She also led Indonesia's bid to join the OECD. Bringing OECD members up to date on her country's reform journey since the Asian Financial Crisis was, she says, "quite eye-opening for many".

"There have been massive and fundamental changes in Indonesia's economic governance since the Reformasi and it is still continuing," she says, citing trade and investment policies, anti-corruption measures and the evolution to an open democracy. "We now share these foundations with OECD countries, but I think many have not been well informed."

Indonesia was stigmatised as a low-income country, Sri Mulyani observes. The country is hell-bent on ridding itself of that stigma. All three presidential candidates in 2024 supported the "Golden Indonesia" goal, which envisages the country hitting high-income status by 2045. This would equate to income per capita of around US$25,000. Indonesia is on track to pass US$5000 per capita this year, however it remains a nation of extreme contrasts. In Jakarta, middle-class parents jostle to get their children into their choice of private school, but more than one-third of people nationwide are economically insecure, meaning a shock can easily tip them into poverty.

The Finance Ministry says consumption alone is enough to ensure Indonesian GDP continues to grow at 5 per cent per annum. Prabowo has more ambitious plans, though: he has promised growth as high as

8 per cent. To get there, Indonesia requires more reform, Sri Mulyani warned shortly after the election. "Our investment needs cannot be met by internal savings, so we need to continue to attract capital," she said. "Investment will come when industry is relatively well developed, when policy is relatively predictable, and when bureaucracy does not become an obstacle."

Sri Mulyani won plaudits for steadying the ship, particularly during the pandemic. To fund emergency spending, the government temporarily relaxed the deficit ceiling imposed more than twenty years ago, which limited borrowing by keeping the budget deficit below 3 per cent of GDP.

Prabowo has suggested it could be time to loosen up fiscal policy. Given the healthy state of the economy, further investments in health and education would be popular. But one essential plank of a developed – or even a stable – nation is still weak. Indonesia's ratio of tax revenue to GDP was just 11 per cent in 2021. This is one of the lowest in the world. The OECD average is around 34 per cent.

Huge swathes of businesses and individuals pay no direct tax, due to the exceptions made for people with low incomes, micro-businesses and many ventures in the health and education sectors, and the unofficial exceptions that apply to informal or unregistered businesses. The Finance Ministry estimates that no tax is paid on 47 per cent of economic activity.

One of Prabowo's key campaign promises was to provide fresh milk and meals for schoolchildren. His campaign team suggested this could cost up to 400 trillion rupiah ($39 billion). To help fund this, the new president has vowed to increase the tax to GDP ratio to 16 per cent, and has pledged to carve revenue collection out of the finance ministry and allocate it to a separate agency. It is not clear how the new collection agency would broaden the tax base. What is clear is the need for a dedicated reformer to continue battling the many vested interests opposed to increasing the tax take. These include the uber-wealthy, whom Sri Mulyani referred to as the crazy rich Indonesians, and the many legislators who believe there should still be more exemptions for low- and middle-income earners.

Speaking in Jakarta soon after the election, Sri Mulyani responded carefully when asked about the future. "It all depends on the president and vice president," she said. "They will look at the challenges ahead and choose who they think are the right people for those challenges."

A day later, a member of Prabowo's campaign team's expert council was more direct. Drajad Wibowo said the finance minister and Prabowo were "not on the same frequency" and had different views on how to fund development. In addition to Prabowo's determination to increase spending on defence, he is also committed to making Indonesia self-sufficient in food staples, particularly rice. He also wants to increase the production of cassava and sugarcane as sources of bioenergy, to boost Indonesia's energy independence. These policies, tapping again into Indonesia's rich reservoir of economic nationalism, resonate with voters. In contrast, Drajad said, Sri Mulyani and her colleagues have not prioritised food and energy: "For them, if imports are cheaper, it is better to import because it is more efficient for the economy."

Prabowo's team has already floated the names of some potential candidates for the key ministry. In addition to health minister Budi Gunadi Sadikin, the Prabowo team is also understood to be considering the chairman of the Financial Services Authority, Mahendra Siregar.

It could be that Prabowo's chest-thumping nationalism will be accompanied by a quiet continuation of fiscal and macroeconomic discipline and market-friendly changes that have served the country well.

Prabowo's Indonesia

Many in the West hope Prabowo will lean towards diversification in foreign partnerships and investments. In recent years, Chinese firms and state actors have ploughed billions into the country's new industrial parks and big-ticket infrastructure projects such as the Whoosh high-speed rail link between Bandung and Jakarta. Some ministers in the Jokowi government, including the de facto prime minister, Luhut Binsar Pandjaitan, had substantial networks in China before entering cabinet, and these connections have played a role as Indonesia went looking for development partners.

This could change quite quickly, said one minister. "To date, it's been China that's willing to sign the cheques. I think the new government will be very open to other players."

The Just Energy Transition Partnership (JETP), launched at the COP26 Summit by South Africa and the International Partners Group, could help shift the balance. This is a plan by G7 countries to marshal US$20 billion to help pay for Indonesia's transition from one of the world's dirtiest economies, powered by coal, oil and gas, to one that runs on green fuel. So far progress has been slow. While Indonesia has delivered a plan, negotiations on financing are ongoing. Last year Jokowi questioned the commitment of the JETP's backers towards Indonesia's energy transition. Progress is likely to be further delayed by the US election.

OECD membership could also come in handy as Jakarta looks to broaden its investor pool. In the past, the Indonesian Investment Authority has grumbled that OECD members only want to invest in other OECD countries. Rather than pursuing its own path to development, Indonesia has now opted to join the club. But it's not a done deal.

In 2021, Jokowi pushed through unpopular labour reforms after the World Bank advised that Indonesia was losing out because regional alternatives like Vietnam were easier to do business with. Will the new president prioritise falling in line with the OECD requirements – particularly if he dispenses with Sri Mulyani, who did so much to get the OECD accession talks over the line?

Many pondering the future take heart from Prabowo's proven pragmatism. Analysts note that uncertainty has increased, but are still assuming that economic policy will remain largely unchanged when Jokowi departs.

Those working to improve Australia's trade and investment links with its northern neighbour will be hoping that assumption is borne out. If Indonesia continues what the OECD describes as its "ambitious reform journey", there is a reasonable chance that more Australians will discover there is a lot more to modern Indonesia than a holiday in Bali. That would be a good outcome for both countries. ■

GROWING PAINS

Can Indonesia rise before its population ages?

Maria Monica Wihardja

Indonesia's election dust has settled, with the ex-military general once accused of human rights abuses and consequently fired from the military, Prabowo Subianto, now minister of defence, set to take over the government in October 2024 with his running mate, President Joko Widodo's 36-year-old son, Gibran Rakabuming Raka. Considering Prabowo's strong ties to the Suharto family, Indonesia's politics seems to be swinging full circle.

Experienced observers such as Ben Bland and Marcus Mietzner might be right in saying that Indonesia is unlikely to go back to an authoritarian government, at least not *de jure*. A Prabowo presidency is unlikely to be an emulation of the New Order, and Prabowo is *not* Suharto. If anything, Jokowi – a man with an uncomplicated public persona but a complex and shrewd mind – has a closer resemblance to Suharto, the smiling general, than Prabowo.

Indonesia has come a long way in improving the quality of its institutions, moving from a 32-year dictatorship synonymous with KKN or *Korupsi, Kolusi dan Nepotisme* (corruption, collusion and nepotism) to a democracy in which five direct presidential elections have been held since 2004. But this progress has been undercut by the recent entrenchment of oligarchy, democratic backsliding and blatant electoral misconduct. Indonesia will perhaps continue to be an electoral democracy but its current state is what game theorists call a "low-equilibrium" outcome, in which no one has the incentive to deviate from the current rules of the game, especially the oligarchy, but everyone could be better off if they chose a different pathway. Breaking this vicious cycle is likely to be difficult, comparable to the fall of the 32-year Suharto regime in 1998 or the coup d'état in 1965. The question is how to put Indonesia on a high-equilibrium trajectory without any major disruptions.

Although policymakers talk about avoiding the middle-income trap, Indonesia has been trapped as a middle-income country for the past thirty years. For decades, about half of Indonesians have aspired to be part of the middle class but lack economic security. Indonesia's working-age population is set to shrink in the next ten years. About 60 per cent of its workforce hasn't completed high school, while around 75 per cent of jobs are in the informal sector. This, in turn, makes many Indonesians economically vulnerable. A poverty assessment report by the World Bank in 2023 found that, in 2019, 40 per cent of Indonesians were "economically insecure", with most of them being "non-poor" (that is, having consumption levels above the US$3.20 per person, per day International Poverty Line) but when exposed to an economic shock, they can easily fall into poverty.

Touted as an emerging power, Indonesia is militarily and economically weak, even compared to its neighbours, but it has the potential to play a greater role on the global stage if it maintains its democracy, stability and development. Its adherence to the non-alignment foreign policy of "rowing between two reefs" has given it a unique position from which to exercise strategic autonomy and to play a mediator role in a world that is becoming increasingly polarised. However, with democratic backtracking, increasing instability and laggard development, the fourth-most populous country and the largest Muslim-majority country in the world could instead be a liability for its neighbours and the world. Poverty can breed social instability and even Islamic extremism.

In less than fifteen years, Indonesia's demography will start to weigh down the nation's economic growth

The question is *how* Indonesia can be an asset rather than a liability for its neighbours and the world.

The next decade

Indonesia is enjoying resilient economic growth, coasting through 5 per cent annual real GDP growth across the past fifteen years (it came back to this 5 per cent trajectory just two years after the COVID-19 pandemic hit in 2020). This rate is, however, not fast enough to bring Indonesia to high-income status before its demographic window of opportunity closes. In less than fifteen years, Indonesia's demography will start to weigh down the nation's economic growth.

In 2022, for every two working-age adults, there was one dependent person, either a child (below fifteen years old) or an older person (sixty-five years or older). But in about fifteen years, or even earlier, the proportion of older dependents will start to increase. The process of ageing, which is reinforced by longer life expectancy and a declining fertility rate, is irreversible: very few countries or societies have become younger once they start to age.

The rate of economic decline will depend on the foundation that the earlier, younger high-growth economy was able to lay, with good health and schooling outcomes, skill formation, labour productivity, infrastructure and strong institutions. This is why the next decade will be so critical. The ageing population is a sign of Indonesians' longer lives and better health, but it will also be a ticking time bomb if Indonesia fails to invest in necessary reforms in time.

Whether Indonesia has reaped or wasted its demographic dividend is debatable. However, as the share of the working-age population declines, Indonesia must move the workforce into higher-productivity sectors and jobs, as well as mobilising the savings that the current cohort of older people have put away or invested when they were younger into productive investment for the next generations. But high rates of chronic malnutrition among children under five years old, poor learning outcomes, a lack of good jobs, and incipient pension and insurance systems remain the greatest challenges for this soon-to-be-ageing society.

According to the World Bank's Human Capital Index 2020, which uses health and education outcomes to predict future productivity, Indonesian children will live up to only 54 per cent of their full productivity potential, compared to 88 per cent for Singaporean children and 69 per cent for Vietnamese children. Scarring effects from the high, albeit declining, "stunting" rate (this is the impaired growth and development that children experience due to poor nutrition, repeated infection and inadequate psychosocial stimulation; it was 22 per cent in 2022) have dragged Indonesia's long-term potential growth down since the 2000s. Although Indonesian children complete 12.4 years of schooling by age eighteen, actual learning was estimated to be only 7.8 years of schooling. Around 53 per cent of ten-year-old children in Indonesia cannot read and understand an age-appropriate text, which is about 19 percentage points higher than the average for the East Asia and Asia-Pacific regions.

A host of issues continue to mire Indonesia's education system and learning outcomes. These include poor quality of teachers, which results in poor quality of education, politicised appointments (and over-hiring) of teachers at the local level, along with elements of corruption and lack of transparency, high rates of teacher absenteeism, and lack of funding and autonomy in the tertiary education sector. The fact that tertiary education is expensive is not helped by Indonesia's low public spending – only 0.3 per cent of GDP – compared to Singapore (1.1 per cent), Malaysia (1.7 per cent) and Vietnam (1.2 per cent). Currently, the sector is highly privatised, and Indonesia does not have a large-scale higher education loan system. Moreover, Indonesia has very restrictive trade and investment barriers in the education sector, although this is slowly changing.

COVID-19 further robbed Indonesia of its demographic dividend. Excess deaths in Indonesia were estimated to reach 736,000, five times the officially reported COVID-19 toll. The pandemic not only caused learning loss because of school closures, but also widened the gaps between poorer and richer students. A World Bank estimate shows that Indonesian fourth graders in 2023 lost eleven months of learning for both maths and language studies, but students from poor households lost eighteen and twenty-seven months. Lower competencies in maths in Indonesia cause an estimated 31 per cent lifetime loss of earnings for men and 39 per cent for women compared to what it would have been without the pandemic.

Indonesia has not been creating the types of jobs that enable the middle-class way of living needed to fuel a middle-class country, let alone a high-income country. Skill formation is also lagging, given many Indonesian children start poorly, as shown by the country's poor education outcomes. Around 75 per cent of Indonesian jobs are informal, largely dominated by employment in gig work such as driving or household enterprises such as smallholding farms and mom-and-pop stores, and they are neither stable nor protect workers.

Indonesia should create more formal jobs that pay decent wages, are stable and protected by labour law (including the minimum wage requirement), offer worker protection benefits and have written contracts. The manufacturing, ICT, finance, health and education sectors are among the most suited to the creation of formal and secure jobs.

The pandemic worsened the labour market transformation process. Indonesia's unemployment rate went up from 5.2 per cent to 7.1 per cent from 2019 to 2020. Many workers switched jobs, changing to more vulnerable types of employment, and experienced reduced incomes. By March 2023, as the worst effects of COVID-19 were coming to an end, a third of Indonesian workers were earning less than before the pandemic.

Indonesia will be ill-prepared to provide for the looming numbers of retirees

Workers in informal and low-end service sectors, including low-end retail, transport and restaurants, were hardest hit. Young people (those aged fifteen to twenty-four) were particularly hard hit, because they were deprived of job opportunities when making the transition from education to work, or because they worked in vulnerable sectors.

Another challenge for the soon-to-be-ageing Indonesia is that it does not yet have mature and well-functioning pension and insurance systems to allow workers to save for their retirement and to allow their savings to be used for productive investments. The latest available data (from 2015) shows that only 14 per cent of the eligible population benefit from an old-age pension in Indonesia, compared to 83 per cent in Thailand in 2016. The vast majority of Indonesians therefore depend on family support, savings and, if they are lucky, investments. Most are not registered in the government's system because they are informal workers, but even those who are registered might not be enrolled in the pension scheme. Indonesia's pension fund's ratio of assets to GDP was only 2 per cent, compared to 105 per cent for OECD countries and 94 per cent for Singapore in 2021. As a result, Indonesia will be ill-prepared to provide for the looming numbers of retirees. Yet social changes, such as changing women's aspirations, will weaken traditional family-based support for the older population, which suggests that pension and insurance systems will have to play a bigger role in economic security.

There are, however, challenges facing the development of the pension and insurance systems, including the large informal sector and the relatively low income per capita, as well as the limited number of long-term investment assets in the domestic market to manage the asset-liability structures and risk exposures. The latter is the consequence of Indonesia's relatively shallow financial and capital markets. Pension and insurance funds currently rely heavily on the yields of the ten-year sovereign bond of the country as a long-term and liquid investment option. However, this does not generate high returns or investment diversification.

New opportunities

Indonesia will also face the challenge of finding new sources of economic growth. It needs to grow by 7–8 per cent annually, instead of 5 per cent, for the next fifteen to twenty years to achieve its dream of becoming a high-income country by its 100th anniversary in 2045. Indonesia's president-elect, Prabowo, has vowed 8 per cent growth. The question remains how Indonesia can close this growth deficit.

The Indonesian government has identified three main engines that will support 5.6–6.1 per cent growth in the next five years, namely the blue economy (marine-based activities such as fisheries), industrialisation, and the tourism and creative industry. The blue economy is still in its initial implementation stage, while the tourism and creative industry is largely concentrated in low-end services. To industrialise, Indonesia is currently "obsessed" with its "downstream" strategy for processing twenty-one commodities in the next two decades. This bans exports of raw critical minerals in order to attract investment in downstream industry such as nickel smelters.

This industrialisation policy follows the development model based on exports and industry, which was key to the success of Japan and the four "Asian Tigers", Singapore, Taiwan, South Korea and Hong Kong. However, it might not be possible to emulate this model anymore. China's rise as the world's sole manufacturing superpower, with a production capacity that is higher than that of the nine next-largest global producers, makes it difficult to compete with. As China's recent success in green technology shows, its wide and deep industrial base gives it the competitive advantage in almost all manufacturing industries.

Perhaps the biggest challenge yet is the ominous potential breakdown of the multilateral trading system, as evident in the dysfunctional dispute settlement body of the World Trade Organization (WTO). Consequently, there has been unrestrained proliferation of protectionist industrial policies across the world, including tax credits and subsidies to attract investment at home ("onshoring") or to those of strategic partners ("nearshoring" or "friendshoring"). As a result, countries are not looking towards offshore manufacturing, as they once did, and investment flows are increasingly concentrated among countries that are geopolitically aligned. Automation also means fewer jobs in the manufacturing sector.

Indonesia has prematurely deindustrialised since the Asian Financial Crisis of 1997–98. Manufacturing's contribution to GDP per capita declined from 32 per cent in 2002 to 19 per cent in 2023. This is because the growth of the manufacturing sector has been slower than that of other sectors and the overall economy. Manufacturing is also not as dynamic as it was before the Asian Financial Crisis, with fewer new firms entering the sector, while the growth of some industries such as tobacco and textiles has slowed.

Re-industrialisation is key to creating middle-class jobs. The manufacturing sector was the largest contributor to the expansion of middle-class jobs in Indonesia between 2011 and 2018, but the present industrial policies have shown no sign of being favourable to middle-class job creation. The share of jobs with a middle-class income has declined since 2016 (see Figure 1), while there has been an increase in the number of those who are neither poor nor vulnerable but who still lack the economic security (mostly because of unstable jobs) to join the middle class. This is a serious threat to Indonesia's economy and welfare.

Figure 1: The share of jobs with a middle-class income (%), 2013–23

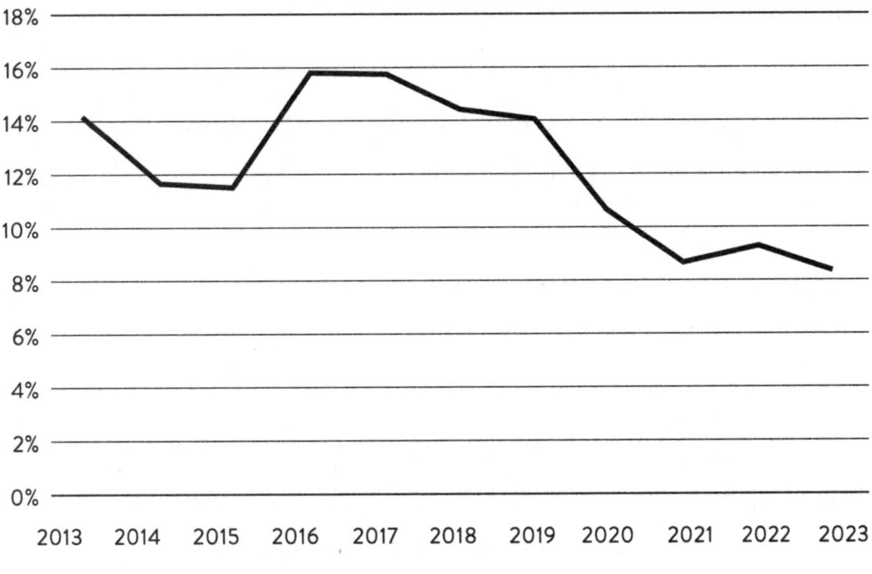

Source: SAKERNAS; author's calculations

Indonesia's strategy of downstreaming critical minerals will not create many jobs, since the relevant industry is very land- and capital-intensive but not labour-intensive. Despite Indonesia's much-lauded success in attracting investment in nickel smelters and boosting nickel-related exports from US$5.3 billion in 2018 to US$30.5 billion in 2022, which includes trade revenues from nickel, nickel products and stainless steel, Indonesia's downstream policy has many drawbacks. This industry creates irreversible environmental costs that are often not considered in the cost-benefit analysis. Moreover, unless the economic benefits received for land and exclusive privileges over natural resources from the commodity export boom are earmarked for developmental projects, like in the 1970s and 1980s, the economic benefits from Indonesia's industrialisation might not trickle down through the whole of society. Moreover, export restriction of raw materials or intermediate inputs will only accelerate the rate of substitution, encouraging producers elsewhere to find alternatives to the raw materials, such as avoiding the use of nickel by switching from nickel-cobalt-manganese battery cells to lithium-iron-phosphate battery cells. Meanwhile, Indonesia has no plan to stop expanding its production capacity despite a supply glut.

Indonesia is right to be seizing new economic opportunities in emerging sectors such as electric vehicles (EVs). Although Indonesia has attracted less investment in the chip industry than neighbours such as Malaysia, Singapore, Vietnam and the Philippines, since it does not have the production capacity, it gains tremendously from foreign investment in EV supply chains and data and artificial intelligence centres. For example, the US chipmaker Nvidia and Indonesia's telecommunication company Indosat Ooredoo Hutchison plan to build a US$200-million artificial intelligence centre in Solo, Central Java.

Yet Indonesia does not need to build whole industries, such as for EVs, as it can specialise in specific parts. It needs to nail down its place in the reconfiguration of the global supply chain as firms and countries de-risk, for instance, by reducing reliance on Chinese trade. It needs to find its competitive advantage in low-carbon industries, the digital economy and the chip industry, prioritising those that could create more and better jobs.

Indonesia's commitment to net-zero carbon emissions by 2060 is a major pledge

Indonesia could also tap into the service sector for its new source of growth. One area that offers a promising future is "digital service exports", involving supplies of services delivered remotely over computer networks. Such services could range from the outsourcing of back-office operations, including data entry and call centres, to programming and web content services intermediated via digital platforms, to chip design. Globally, there is growing demand for digital service exports.

In summary, Indonesia must diversify its exports and economy, which continue to rely heavily on natural resources, and move towards a more knowledge-based economy, including high-end services. Government policies to achieve this may include the upskilling of workers, the removal of restrictions on competition and foreign investment in the services sector, and the creation of an environment conducive to growing the emerging sectors of digital service exports and low-carbon industries.

Leading in the global climate transition

Since Indonesia is the largest archipelagic country in the world – it has some 17,000 islands – rising sea levels and other climate change events will pose serious, and even existential, threats to its population. Every year, mean sea levels increase by 0.8–1.2 centimetres, and there are 42 million people living in low-lying areas of Indonesia below ten metres above sea level, who are highly vulnerable to sea level rise. USAID has projected that 2000 small islands could be submerged because of the sea level rise by 2050. The number of natural disasters, such as floods and droughts, has increased by 7 per cent annually since 2012. Between 2020 and 2024, Indonesia's average economic loss due to climate change amounted to US$7.3 billion per year.

Indonesia's commitment to net-zero carbon emissions by 2060 is a major pledge. Indonesia is among the top ten largest carbon-emission countries, contributing around 2 per cent of global emissions in 2020. Around 60 per cent of the country's energy industry is still based on non-renewable sources, such as coal. Aside from energy, the other main contributor to Indonesia's emissions is forestry and peatland fires due mainly to deforestation, though emissions from these have decreased significantly over the past five years.

The good news is that economic growth has shown signs of decoupling from the growth of greenhouse-gas emissions. The bad news is that financing the transition towards net zero and green energy remains a significant task.

One of the main challenges in financing the green economy is a lack of global agreement on what are considered "green economic activities". The most contentious criterion is whether the phasing-out of coal power plants can be considered "green" activities. Through Indonesia's state-owned electricity company, PLN, there is currently an oversupply of coal-powered electricity in Java and Bali. But PLN has existing long-term agreements to buy power from coal-fired plants. Unless PLN can reimburse these plants for their early retirement, it will be difficult to transition from coal to renewable sources. Indonesia has been spearheading global moves to consider the early retirement of coal plants as a green economic activity.

Total investment in "green assets" is dire. Indonesia could develop its pension and insurance sectors to increase the availability of funds for long-term green investments. However, Indonesia's pension and insurance sectors are still very incipient. Moreover, less than 2 per cent of total bonds outstanding in 2021 can be classified as green bonds. One issue is that there is no "green-mium" – that is, no extra return for investing in green projects compared to "brown" projects. The national government recently passed the *Law on Financial Sector Development and Strengthening,* whose chief objective is to overhaul the insurance and pension fund sectors, which is necessary for building Indonesia's domestic financing capacity so that the country can meet its global climate change commitments.

Distortionary policies and incentives hamper efforts to reduce Indonesia's emissions. These policies include huge subsidies for coal-fired power plants and an absence of measures that disincentivise environmentally damaging projects, such as a carbon tax and pricing mechanisms. There are also regulations that favour environmentally damaging projects, such as the removal of coal pollution from the list of hazardous industrial emissions in 2021, and incentives for nickel smelters that are largely powered by coal generation. These policies, plus Indonesia's local content requirement policy, make investment in renewable energy less attractive.

Reforms are incomplete

If Indonesia is serious about becoming a high-income country by 2045, it must improve the quality of its institutions. Despite some progress, reforms have been fickle, as recently shown by Indonesia's drastically worsened corruption and democratic backsliding, significantly due to resistance by an entrenched oligarchy. These could threaten Indonesia's long-term growth. Importantly, because Indonesia's political system is financed by political parties and oligarchs, productivity-seeking innovation often finds itself overshadowed by rent-seeking activities, which ultimately hinders the prospects for economic growth.

Indonesia's efforts to join international organisations and forums provide a valuable opportunity to improve its institutions, especially its judicial, anti-corruption and law-enforcement bodies, as well as agencies addressing climate change and environmental compliance. Accession to international organisations can "lock in" difficult reforms by embedding domestic policies in an international institution. Indonesia's membership of the WTO, the G20 and the United Nations Framework Convention on Climate Change for example, has helped it to align closer to international standards and improve governance. The reforms Indonesia made after the Asian Financial Crisis of 1997–98 – which included a 3 per cent fiscal deficit limit and 60 per cent debt-to-GDP ratio limit, and the adoption of risk-based banking supervision – have helped it maintain economic stability and resilience in the past two decades. More recently, accession to the Financial Action Task Force in 2023 requires Indonesia to align its legislation, policies and practices with international standards in combating money laundering.

Indonesia's decision this year to accede to the OECD is therefore a step in the right direction, since it may spur Jakarta to lock in its nascent reforms. Indonesia's application for membership is ambitious, as it involves aligning the nation's domestic policies with the OECD's 268 legal instruments. The challenge will be greatest in the areas of corruption (including bribery in international trade licensing), environmental compliance, tax crimes, trans-border data flows, corporate governance in state-owned enterprises, labour standards, trade openness, as well as reinforcing democracy. These reforms will be politically costly in the short run.

> **There is much uncertainty surrounding the economic policies of a Prabowo presidency**

Indeed, the accession process is not merely technical but decidedly political – domestically and between individual nations. Past accessions show that OECD member countries sometimes provide political backing for successful accession. Hence, Indonesia will also need to engage in strategic diplomacy. The United States, the United Kingdom and Australia are among the thirty-three countries that have shown support for Indonesia's accession, while Israel has raised objections.

It may be too early to tell whether president-elect Prabowo will continue to support the accession or whether he will withdraw and revert to the à la carte pattern of cooperation. It will also depend on how much political capital Prabowo is willing to invest in laborious institutional reforms, given he is likely to face resistance from within his "rainbow" cabinet.

Can Indonesia benefit its neighbours?

The enormous size and potential of Indonesia's economy and market mean it can be a big asset to its neighbours, including Australia. However, Indonesia's economy continues to rely on the boom and bust of commodity cycles. It muddles through difficult economic and political episodes, but this is not enough to bring it to high-income status by 2045.

Indonesia is racing against time to graduate to high-income status before its soon-to-be ageing population weighs the economy down. Indonesia's current economic performance is similar to that of middle-income neighbours such as the Philippines, Malaysia and Thailand, but seems to be lagging behind Vietnam's.

To succeed, Indonesia will need to cement its competitive advantage in the changing global supply chains and emerging industries, and ensure that its spending does not get too loose amid rising populist policies under Prabowo's presidency.

Indonesia should continue to have productive dialogues with trading partners and take advantage of its existing partnership agreements, including with Australia. For example, the Indonesia–Australia Comprehensive Economic Partnership Agreement has provisions that aim to improve Indonesian health professional standards and vocational education and training, as well as higher education. Its agreement to help achieve a US$2-trillion digital economy target in ASEAN can bring opportunities to Indonesia's digital economy. And its agreement with the United States could help it earn trust on technology transfers – for example, in the chip industry – and plug into US supply chains.

After the ten-year presidency of Jokowi, there is much uncertainty surrounding the economic policies of a Prabowo presidency. Prabowo is likely to adopt populist economic policies, such as those announced in his election campaign, including the "iconic" free lunch and milk program, increasing salaries for civil servants, food self-sufficiency, the renovating of school buildings, as well as hospital construction in each regency, and even perhaps free tertiary education. Eventually, his election rhetoric will hit the hard reality of limited fiscal space, which can be partly eased by phasing out the expensive but highly popular fuel subsidies and increasing the relatively low ratio of tax revenues to GDP. His "realist" approach to defence and foreign policy might also mean burgeoning defence and military spending. To achieve his 8 per cent growth target, he might have to trade economic stability for higher growth.

A number of key markers will indicate whether Prabowo's presidency is likely to achieve the reforms Indonesia direly needs for the next decade: cabinet appointments, major policy and institutional changes, such as the relaxation of the fiscal deficit limit of 3 per cent and the establishment of the State Revenue Board, as well as policy responses to geopolitical tensions, climate change and technological advancement.

Prabowo's power consolidation in the parliament – that is, whether his coalition reaches a majority – will determine whether he can be unbounded in his policymaking. Having said that, his economic policy will have limits. The market and investors can "punish" poor policy by taking their investment out of Indonesia and/or raising risk perception (causing higher yields and costs of financing). Indonesia's commitments to international institutions such as the Financial Action Task Force and ASEAN will also put a limit on regulatory divergence from international standards. Lastly, Indonesia is becoming a more mature, albeit still young, democracy, so voters – especially those of the more educated middle class – will continue to be vocal and critical of the government's policymaking.

A more prosperous Indonesia will be an asset to its neighbours. Hence, helping Indonesia accelerate its development and institutional reforms should be a goal that Canberra and Jakarta share. ■

THE FIX *Solving Australia's foreign affairs challenges*

Bart Hogeveen and Gatra Priyandita on Why Australia Should Lead an Indo-Pacific Cyber Peacekeeping Effort

"A standing joint operation of cybersecurity and defence agencies would … cement people-to-people links between professionals, build confidence and trust between the governments involved, and encourage 'on-the-job' improvement of skills, techniques and competencies."

THE PROBLEM: Cyber and technology capabilities are at the heart of strategic competition and the global arms race. Whichever nation manages to acquire an edge in emerging sensitive and critical technologies will be able to exert lasting economic, diplomatic and military influence over its allies and partners as well as over its foes and competitors. Ensuring that cyber and technology, as tools of statecraft, are used responsibly demands a major diplomatic surge.

In the Indo-Pacific, the rapid growth in cyber capabilities has encouraged states to achieve economic and strategic goals through cyber operations, frequently in a coercive manner. State agencies are involved, but more often they rely on the tacit support of proxy groups such as commercial service providers, crime syndicates and patriotic hackers.

These hackers – who often have multiple and changing allegiances – exploit weaknesses in networks of critical infrastructure, steal innovation secrets and engage in information warfare. They're also involved in the online suppression of dissidents and free speech, and in the multibillion-dollar cybercrime market.

These cyber threats are inherently transnational. But when it comes to our region's approach to prevention, it's every state for itself. While there are examples of international support after major incidents, such as when Tonga was affected by a cable outage and Vanuatu's government experienced ransomware attacks in 2022, such cooperation has generally focused on containing the issue and restoring systems. However, the constant and persistent character of most of these cybersecurity threats remains ignored.

The Medibank and Optus data breaches in Australia showed that malicious cyber activities can affect people's lives dramatically. And they can disturb high-income countries as much as emerging economies and developing nations.

Decades of diplomatic negotiations have convinced states to refrain from the most disastrous actions while taking responsibility for due diligence on their territory, and to commit to cooperation. However, these agreements have not been accompanied by mechanisms for assessing violations or for promoting compliance and accountability – in particular when it involves states unwilling and/or unable to halt cybercrime operations originating from their territory. In fact, the gap between states that can address major transnational cybersecurity issues on their own and those that can't has widened.

In November 2023, the Albanese government launched Australia's fourth cybersecurity strategy, which expresses the government's aim to lead globally in upholding international law and norms, and to shape future standards. The Department of Foreign Affairs and Trade (DFAT) plans to invest $47.4 million to establish rapid-response teams to assist Pacific nations with major cyber incidents, to help them reduce their vulnerabilities, and to improve their responses to incidents in South-East Asia. But this is not enough.

THE PROPOSAL: Australia needs to assert itself as a middle power in cyberspace. And it can do so by becoming the first Indo-Pacific cyber peacekeeper. As cyberspace becomes a contested domain of international relations, states need to work out permanent structures for dialogue and communication; for the detection, monitoring and analysis of threats; for taking preventive or retributive actions; and for building the resilience necessary to preserve a peaceful digital environment, particularly for those nations that are most fragile.

How can Australia become a cyber peacekeeper? First, Canberra should elevate cybersecurity and cyber defence cooperation on the agenda of its main multilateral and minilateral forums, including ASEAN Plus, the ASEAN Regional Forum, the Pacific Islands Forum, the Quad, the G20 and MIKTA. It should use these forums to establish a permanent dialogue on cybersecurity incidents and develop shared assessments of risks, threats and appropriate responses. Eight years ago, Singapore initiated a regular annual meeting of ministers responsible for cybersecurity among the ASEAN members. Australia could build on this and expand it into a regional council of cybersecurity ministers. Learning from other conflict-prevention measures, like the Workshop on Managing Potential Conflicts in the South China Sea, such a permanent dialogue should include a Track II component in which governments and the expert community work together.

Australia should also work with other cyber-capable countries – such as Singapore, South Korea, Japan, Malaysia, potentially the United Kingdom and the United States, and perhaps even the People's Republic of China – to establish a permanent operational structure for a cyber peacekeeping effort, similar to the combined maritime forces that deal with piracy in the Western Indian Ocean. This peacekeeping effort should encompass detecting, monitoring and analysing cybersecurity threats that affect the most vulnerable assets in the region, and – in extremis – might initiate action to block such threats. The cyber peacekeepers can be expected to encounter cybercrime syndicates, contract hackers and malign nation-states, and should be equipped to protect people, businesses and infrastructure from the most common forms of cybersecurity threats.

A standing joint operation of cybersecurity and defence agencies would bring additional benefits. It would cement people-to-people links between professionals, build confidence and trust between the governments involved, and encourage "on-the-job" improvement of skills, techniques and competencies.

Finally, Australia should secure industry support and technical expertise, and offer support packages in infrastructure, hardware, software and policy practices at "mates' rates". For this, Australia should expand its corps of cybersecurity experts qualified to operate in regional and developmental contexts. The Australian cybersecurity industry has a lot to offer, but their current focus on high-end cybersecurity services alienates them from South-East Asian and Pacific customers.

WHY IT WILL WORK: When great powers are at odds with each other, and when the rules of the game are ignored, it is up to middle powers to step up. Cyber peacekeeping offers an opportunity for Indo-Pacific governments to collaborate, provide operational support to one another and share expertise. And confronting cybercrime and ICT vulnerabilities is an area in which the interests of these governments, including China's, converge.

There's a great economic incentive too. Australia's economy is increasingly intertwined with that of the Indo-Pacific. The digitisation of trade and commerce in South and South-East Asia and the Pacific is opening up new markets, and the region is a growing source of cyber talent in a job market marked by shortages. Almost every state in the Indo-Pacific now has an established national cybersecurity or defence agency. Together, these institutions should be able to sustain the operational needs that a cyber peacekeeping effort would require. There is every reason for Australia to look for ways to share the burden of cybersecurity prevention, finding economies of scale and pooling the skills of the region's cyberdefence professionals.

Finally, it would be an opportunity for Prime Minister Anthony Albanese to follow through on his commitment to be "an exemplary partner" to the countries of South-East Asia; to support the Pacific's regional security agenda; and to achieve his government's aim of upholding international norms and standards.

An Australian-led cyber peacekeeping operation would be a bold and unprecedented step, but it has the potential to positively affect people's and businesses' sense of cybersafety, to win the hearts and minds of cybersecurity and defence leaders, and to expedite digital transformation across the region. And yes, this could involve China as well. ■

Reviews

India Is Broken: A People Betrayed, Independence to Today
Ashoka Mody
Stanford University Press

India polarises like few other places. Visitors either revel in the life and colour or recoil from the tumult and inequality.

It does similar things to analysts of the country's politics and economy. Some become convinced that India is an emerging giant destined to reshape our world and others come to see it as a land of perpetual social crisis, sliding towards autocracy and stagnation.

Ashoka Mody, a distinguished Indian-born economist now an American citizen, and a former official at the International Monetary Fund and the World Bank, sits squarely in the second camp. He thinks India is "broken". India's economy, he believes, is unable to provide the millions of decent jobs ordinary people need to provide for themselves and to live with dignity. Its politics are increasingly authoritarian and violent. Its society shows all the signs of "moral decay".

Mody's book aims to explain what went wrong, how and why. It is a compelling read, partly because he does not hide his anger about what he thinks has happened to India since it gained independence in 1947. Nor is he coy about where he believes the blame lies. The villains of his story are the country's politicians. They have eroded social norms, he argues, and taken full advantage of the "decay of political accountability". It is their irresponsibility and venality that have broken India. And if there is a remedy for the country's ills, Mody believes, it lies beyond politics, in the reconstruction of the country's social fabric.

Mody makes this case with a pacy retelling of India's postcolonial history. He starts with Jawaharlal Nehru, the first prime minister, who recognised that unemployment was the most pressing problem, but who also made the first missteps. Nehru ought to have reformed agriculture and boosted manufacturing, Mody argues, but instead opted for "big-push" industrialisation, with heavy industry and large-scale power generation. This strategy came at an increasingly unsustainable financial and human cost. India had to borrow ever larger sums from abroad to make it work. Its politicians grew dependent on a small group of major industrialists entrusted to deliver on their economic plans. Schools remained neglected, agriculture unproductive and jobs scarce.

Things deteriorated further after Nehru's death in 1964. His Congress Party disintegrated into competing factions. Drought led to poor harvests. India was forced to seek foreign financial assistance and food aid. Social cohesion frayed, with lasting consequences. Riots broke out with disturbing frequency, communal violence between religious groups surged, and a large-scale Maoist insurgency flared and festered. Corruption spread, while voters, losing faith in public institutions, transferred their trust to charismatic politicians. For good reason, Mody gives a simple and straightforward title to the section covering the twenty years after Nehru's demise: "Violence".

Indira Gandhi, Nehru's daughter and India's third prime minister, did little to stop the rot. Indeed, she made things worse, despite her promise to "remove poverty" from the country. She stifled the economy with bureaucracy and corruption and flirted with dictatorship. She indulged her wayward son, Sanjay, coercing banks into lending him money for pet projects and appointing him to lead campaigns to clear slums and sterilise millions of poor men to curb population growth. Disastrously, she stoked and exploited separatism in Punjab, leading to her assassination at the hands of her Sikh bodyguards and a decade-long civil conflict that killed thousands.

Mody acknowledges that things improved a little after Indira. He credits her successor, her surviving son, Rajiv, with good ideas, and praises P.V. Narasimha Rao, prime minister during the reform years of 1991–96, for his boldness. But he castigates the political elite of that time for decisions that fanned the flames of Hindu nationalism, for their failure to rein in corruption and for their unwillingness to invest in education.

To this point, Mody's story will be familiar to most readers. Yet what comes next might surprise some of those who have tracked India's ascent to claim the title of the world's fifth-largest economy. Gross domestic product has grown, Mody observes, but for most Indians, all that glitters is not gold. To be sure, the real estate and construction sectors are prospering, along with the politicians and officials trading insider knowledge and permits for personal gain. But those parts of the economy that might provide good jobs and sustainable growth – agriculture and manufacturing – still languish.

In parallel, Mody laments, India's politics have become as toxic as Delhi's winter air. The current government has not just driven the economy "off the edge", he thinks – it has smashed India's "broken democracy" too. Instead of providing public goods, Narendra Modi's Bharatiya Janata Party (BJP) supplies spectacle, drama and "religious exclusion".

Many have arrived at similar conclusions in recent years. And some think the only response to such systematic failure is a dose of Chinese-style authoritarianism, engaging the technocrats to get India back on track without the distractions and temptations of democratic politics.

To his credit, Mody rejects that idea. But what he advocates instead is equally problematic. India's politicians, he thinks, have caused a breakdown in India's moral norms. They have created what he calls a "me-me-me equilibrium", where citizens cheat and scam one another and are cheated and scammed in turn. To fix this, he argues, Indians must rebuild social trust by reviving civic communities led by public-spirited individuals. Then they should transfer this grassroots vigour into local government, restoring integrity and accountability into India's politics from below.

Here Mody leans heavily on the work of Western social theorists like Robert Putnam. But they also echo popular Indian ideas. The argument that the restoration of India will come not from political action but from social reform is a familiar one, made many times since the mid-nineteenth century, most notably by Hindu revivalists, including Vivekananda and Gandhi. Indeed, it animates Hindu nationalist movements such as the Rashtriya

Swayamsevak Sangh (RSS – National Volunteers' Organisation). Formally, at least, the RSS is committed to the restoration of India's social bonds and to the decentralisation of political power.

This parallel does not refute Mody's argument. Quite the opposite. The RSS has flourished since the 1980s, and today boasts 6 million members, including ministers in the Modi government. It provides evidence, perhaps, there is a demand for civic communities in India. But many would contest the suggestion that the success of the RSS has improved the country's politics.

There is a case for saying that India needs a political remedy for its various ills, not a social one. For a start, it has long lacked truly competitive politics at the national level. For almost forty years after 1947, the Congress Party ruled largely unopposed. It had critics, of course, but they either failed to establish a plausible platform from which to challenge Congress or declared themselves uninterested in electoral politics. Today, after a decade in power, India finds itself in a similar situation. A controversial BJP-led government with a contested record faces a fractured and weak opposition, unable to coalesce around a clear agenda or single leader. The most plausible alternative to Narendra Modi, Nehru's great-grandson Rahul Gandhi, is widely considered equivocal about political life. In such circumstances, in any country, integrity and accountability would deliquesce, with all the consequences Mody describes so well.

Ian Hall

DEFENCE

Girt by Sea: Re-imagining Australia's Security
Rebecca Strating
& Joanne Wallis
La Trobe University Press

An observer of the Australian national security scene, considering the mainstream media landscape of the 2010s, might well conclude that there were only a handful of commentators on Australian foreign affairs, and that all were white men of a certain age. Not only were other voices rarely featured, the limited range of items in Australia's big-ticket strategic debates (caused by its geographical position and alliance history) meant the same voices were heard often on the same issues. A closer look, of course, would have revealed a much more diverse pool.

In recent years, this more diverse generation of foreign policy thinkers has been achieving the public recognition it has long deserved (and pushed for, both by producing excellent work and by advocating for the inclusion of a wider range of voices). *Girt by Sea: Re-imagining Australia's Security* shows what happens when experienced but imaginative voices enter the public debate on national security. Drawing on their extensive academic expertise, Rebecca Strating and Joanne Wallis have written a clear, timely and provocative book that focuses on the big national security questions that every Australian should care about.

Strating and Wallis cleverly use Australia's geography as a starting point. Australia is "girt by sea" – or, to be more accurate, six seas. They consider the threats, challenges and opportunities rising on the tides of Australia's "north seas", the Western Pacific, the South China Sea, the South Pacific, the Indian Ocean and the Southern Ocean. Through this lens they consider both Australia's conventional national security issues (its delicate geostrategic balancing between the United States and China) and its unconventional challenges (the range of non-state actors involved in crime and terror, climate change and "grey-zone" threats, or the complex cocktail of threats involving state and non-state actors, occurring somewhere between peace and war).

The decision to focus on these six maritime spaces challenges much Australian strategic thinking right out of the gate. For at least a decade, the "Indo-Pacific" has dominated the debate on Australian national security. Any scepticism about the utility of the concept has not appeared to trouble policymakers, who use the term almost exclusively when speaking about Australia's maritime domain. Strating and Wallis's work demonstrates the dangers of treating Australia's complex maritime neighbourhood as one giant ocean stretching over nearly half the world. They point out that the different components of the Indo-Pacific have different histories and pose different security challenges.

Using the six "seas" as their jumping-off point also allows Strating and Wallis to navigate one of the major challenges of national security commentary: how do we consider "conventional" and "unconventional" threats in a way that acknowledges that these two types of threat are intertwined? Very often the tendency is to focus on one, with a sprinkling of recognition given to the other. But by focusing on the maritime space – where these threats not only coexist but also facilitate each other – Strating and Wallis are able to provide a holistic picture of the national security environment.

The world's oceans present a unique opportunity to analyse unconventional and grey-zone threats. The lack of overarching authority over the high seas and the difficulty of law enforcement mean that organised crime can thrive in the maritime. From piracy and smuggling to illegal, unauthorised and under-regulated fishing, oceans are crucial to the conduct of local and international crime at every level, from the opportunistic to the highly organised. Certain crimes – such as sabotaging undersea cables, or fishing illegally – can be directed by state authorities against their adversaries, as well as by criminals. The same lack of structure that facilitates crime also facilitates grey-zone threats – some of which are simply crimes committed by state authorities.

Crime enforcement is extremely effective cover for states wanting to do something else entirely. This can range from the reasonably innocent – there is little doubt that the enthusiastic international response to Indian Ocean counter-piracy stemmed from strategic enthusiasm to have an excuse to patrol the waters around the Horn of Africa – to the more suspect. Chinese coastguard "enforcement" of fishing rights is simply the dressing-up of geostrategic impulses in a more palatable uniform; Strating and Wallis provide a thorough and effective summary of the issues involved in this "white hull" warfare in their chapter on the South China Sea.

Strating and Wallis's six-seas structure also reveals that the strategic dance Australia must perform to deal with the pressures of US–China competition is not consistent, but varies from region to region. Sharpest in the Western Pacific and the South China Sea, Strating and Wallis argue that this strategic relationship intrudes differently, and often less, in other maritime spaces. There is value in reminding the national security community that the Sino–US security situation plays out differently in different regions: it can help focus Australian resources where they are most needed, and inform a debate about the extent to which – and in which areas – Australia should actively balance against China.

In nearly every section of the book, the question of the health and vitality of the so-called rules-based international order makes an appearance. A focus on the world's oceans means the relevant rule is nearly always the United Nations Convention on the Law of the Sea (UNCLOS). There's no doubt that UNCLOS has significant implications for international order, as it provides for freedom of navigation and facilitates interpretation of national boundaries in the world's oceans. Strating and Wallis argue throughout their six cases that in fact UNCLOS may only be under significant challenge in the South China Sea, and that its utility nearly everywhere else means that even players like China may not have an interest in upending the entire system, just the system as it relates to the South China Sea. (And this, the authors assert, doesn't necessarily challenge the entire international order, but rather seeks an exception related to the South China Sea.) The variability in how and where UNCLOS is challenged is nicely illustrated throughout all the cases in the book. For example, Strating and Wallis note that Peter Dutton – at the time the defence minister – misinterpreted a Chinese action in the Indian Ocean (within Australia's exclusive economic zone) as an "act of aggression", when in fact it was the type of freedom of navigation that Australia staunchly supports elsewhere.

Girt by Sea concludes by sounding some timely warnings for policymakers. A book that focuses on Australia's six maritime domains, all with their own histories, demonstrates through its very existence the complexity of Australia's national security situation. Strating and Wallis argue that Australia has met this complexity with more complexity: there are over twenty relevant Australian agencies and entities dealing with maritime issues. But as a result there is a lack of connected thinking about maritime issues. Throughout the book, the authors explain how climate change will worsen the security situation in each of the six seas, from challenging fisheries and natural resources to posing an existential threat to island nations. They concede that they may be idealistic in assuming that policy thinking can connect national security and climate, but they are not wrong to argue that these issues are connected. Strating and Wallis call for a more coherent national *security* strategy, rather than another defence-led exercise, as one way of linking these disparate areas of thinking.

Sarah Percy

Climate Politics in Oceania: Renewing Australia–Pacific Relations in a Warming World
Edited by Susan Harris Rimmer, Caitlin Byrne & Wesley Morgan
Melbourne University Press

This book's title is apt, given that the climate crisis is increasingly being used to leverage political capital and power, while the planet is dying and people are facing floods, fires, cyclones, droughts, cyclones and other calamities. *Climate Politics in Oceania* is a collection of articles that engage in a kind of consensual dialogue (as opposed to debate) with one another on the nexus between Australia's climate diplomacy, its strategic and security policies, and its relationship with Pacific islands countries.

Collectively, the essays ask pertinent questions about Australia's commitment to carbon emissions reduction, and argue that its approach over the past decade has been "largely characterised by political inertia, policy blind spots and diplomatic isolation". Worse, Australia has been categorised by some as a "climate pariah state", in the same league as Saudi Arabia, China and Brazil. Australia's position contrasts with that of the Pacific islands states, which, according to the introduction by Caitlin Byrne, Wesley Morgan and Susan Harris Rimmer, "offer alternative experiences, narratives and models of climate leadership, including in their leveraging of political opportunity, policy consensus and collective diplomacy".

A major theme of the book is that Australia's climate policies have been compromised by corporate, strategic and other self-serving interests, which undermine its status as a trusted neighbour and partner. The election in May 2022 of a Labor government in Australia was welcomed, but the high expectations turned sour when its policy on phasing out fossil fuels was frustratingly similar to that of the previous Coalition administration. As well as having political ramifications in Australia, this decision has undermined the Pacific regional stance on combating climate change.

The book features academics, practitioners and observers from various areas of expertise, including foreign policy, national security, defence, sociology, science, international law and diplomacy. The diversity of narratives reflects the multidimensional and constantly shifting nature of climate politics, geopolitics and the role of states. Of particular significance, the book challenges the dominant narrative about the vulnerability and helplessness of "backyard" Pacific communities in the face of climate politics. In fact, Pacific islands states are at the forefront of the fight against climate change, while Australia focuses on what the book refers to as "narrow strategic imperatives", such as minerals exports, employment, and facilitating corporate interests and competition with China.

The twelve chapters are linked through the well-written introduction by editors Byrne, Morgan and Harris Rimmer. They identify policy shortcomings, diplomatic blind spots and geopolitical deficits in relation to Australian's engagement with the region. Dame Meg Taylor, former Secretary General of the Pacific Islands Forum (PIF), follows with a broad-brush account of the PIF's regional approach, including the Blue Pacific Continent and associated initiatives.

Simon Bradshaw provides a scientific analysis of the impact of climate change and the need to reduce carbon emissions as a means of mitigating the increasingly destructive cyclones, rising sea levels, droughts, flooding, coral bleaching and other consequences of global warming. The article ends with a sense of hope, however: "Determined action on climate change, informed by the best science coupled with local traditional knowledge, and developed and implemented in true partnership and collaboration, holds the promise of a better future."

This is followed by an article by Byrne, Andrea Haefner and Johanna Nalau on Australia's environment ambassador, a position created in 1989 in what was a pioneering act of climate diplomacy. Despite the diplomatic skills of the environment ambassadors, their work and impact have been hindered by "the narrow casting of Australia's national interests, the dominance of a core set of domestic economic concerns and the politically charged nature of the debates".

Pacific perspectives are then provided by Morgan, George Carter and Fulori Manoa, whose main discursive thrust is to place Pacific agency at the centre of the climate discourse. Over the years, Pacific islands states have been at the forefront of global climate action, while Australia, the authors argue, "has dragged its feet on cutting climate emissions and has at times played a spoiler role in climate change negotiations at the UN".

Next is a report on perceptions of the extent to which climate change features in China's geopolitical and developmental engagement with the region. Among the findings of this empirical research, an emerging view is that there is "minimal engagement between China and Pacific islands countries in relation to mitigation issues". Given that China is a major fossil-fuel producer and user, one does not expect much from the country by way of innovative emissions-reduction strategies.

Brendan Sargeant focuses on Australia's security alliance with the United States. His paper argues that while climate change is now recognised worldwide as an existential security threat to the planet and humanity, this has not been seriously factored into the Australian security and strategic philosophy, and so is a matter of grave concern for the region.

Melissa Conley Tyler provides an optimistic and affirmative view of Australia's new "transformative" approach to regional diplomacy, security and climate change, the result of the current government's engagement strategies in the region. This, Conley Tyler argues, "is an opportunity for Australia's development, diplomacy and defence engagement to work together in an integrated way to build a shared future with the Pacific".

The connection between Australia's strategic culture and climate change is examined further by Mark Beeson, who, like Sargeant, contends that Australia's narrow strategic focus on traditional security overshadows the growing international consensus about the imminent threat of climate change as a major security threat.

Following this, Sandra Tarte explores the background of the contestation of geopolitical narratives in the Pacific. Her article connects the range of regional initiatives on climate change and security, and explains how these have developed over the years.

The final two chapters focus on specific technical issues relating to maritime boundaries and human rights law and their relationships to climate change. Rebecca Strating and Joanne Wallis argue that climate change has direct bearing on maritime boundaries of Pacific islands states, especially as sea levels rise and islands go underwater. This will pose a threat to national sovereignty and the survival of island states. Climate justice and international human rights law, according to Harris Rimmer, should guide Australia's climate diplomacy in the Pacific to "amplify Pacific voices, and a sense of urgency".

The book is a timely reminder to Australia, the PIF's largest member state, that it needs to relinquish its "deputy sheriff" image and adopt a good neighbourly personality, one that supports efforts to reach a regional consensus. Australia is a close American ally and is part of the global US client-state system: its strategic loyalty to that alliance eclipses its commitment to Pacific regional issues. The awkward question to ask here is: does this mean that although Australia is in the Pacific islands region, it is not necessarily part of the Pacific islands community of nations in soul and identity?

The authors in this volume ask penetrating questions about Australia's security designs, diplomatic strategies and climate policies in the region. These questions should resonate in the corridors of power in Canberra. The academics have spoken – now it's the turn of the policymakers to consider and discuss their ideas as they congregate for their Friday-afternoon drinks at the Capitol Bar. More importantly, they must do something in response when they return to work the following Monday morning.

Steven Ratuva

Correspondence

"Fatal Shores" by Hugh White

Peter J. Dean

Australia is an open, democratic society where the contest of ideas is critical, and no more so than in the realm of national security. Hugh White has been a paragon of this discourse in Australia for over two decades, and the sheer scale, audacity and potential impact of AUKUS – the highest-profile and most complex national undertaking by Australia in generations – demands that it receive scrutiny and be contestable. This contest, however, must be based on an evidentiary basis.

White's analysis of the pact between Australia, the United States and the United Kingdom in "Fatal Shores" (Australian Foreign Affairs 20) is not forensic. Unfortunately, it lacks hard evidence to support its claims, relies on inference, skews fact and engages in wordplay, giving little credit to the need for clear contestability or to those who have substantive concerns about the AUKUS deal.

White's analysis of AUKUS is a vehicle to prosecute the strategic argument that he has pursued for over a decade. White's original argument, outlined in his Quarterly Essay *Power Shift* (2010), was an exceptionally important contribution to the national discourse on how Australia should respond to our region's extraordinary strategic changes. It caused the policy community to pause and rethink all their assumptions, and to sharpen their arguments. But White's own argument has not held up. And repackaging it around AUKUS does not change this fact. Instead, the essay continues an analytical line of thought that reduces the Indo-Pacific to a G2 competition between China and the United States, built around the apparent inevitability of China's rise, US decline and Australia's supposed blind support for war with China over Taiwan in a vain attempt to preserve White's continued belief in a US preference for primacy.

This view is reductionist. It removes agency from the multiplicity of states that make up our complex and diverse region, and stands at odds with how the region has evolved since White's argument was first delivered. As Foreign Minister Penny Wong noted in her National Press Club address in 2023: "Many commentators and strategists prefer to look at what is happening in the region simply in terms of great powers competing for primacy. They love a binary. And the appeal of a binary is obvious. Simple, clear choices. Black and white."

To the uninitiated, White's assessment is alluring in its simplicity: AUKUS is too complex and too risky; it locks us into a misguided US strategy against China; and it is being pushed on us by people and organisations that have strategically lost their way. In contrast, White's solution is full of clarity and simplicity, driven by a philosopher's belief in the certainty of their own conviction. But his arguments have attracted little, if any, support among the strategic community, and the prescribed policy solutions have held no sway with governments both near and far.

This is because the essay is designed around a series of straw men. With a few brisk turns of phrase, AUKUS moves from a technology-sharing pact to a security alliance; its focus on key technologies is replaced by a fallacy of British new-age imperialism; nuclear-powered submarines (SSN) turn from a capability of deterrence and denial in the defence of Australia to a platform focused on supporting US carrier battle groups, and the inevitability that a submarine capability must drag Australia into a war alongside the United States that it can't possibly win.

Just as artful are the sweeping statements unsupported by evidence (that Australia will play no discernible role in AUKUS Pillar 2 and the technology will happen anyway); the selective use of evidence (that the original Attack-class submarines were going to cost $100 billion, when the cost was estimated to be $225–245 billion, is a matter of public record); the contradictions (that SSNs are unrealistic for Australia as their crewing requirements are too high, overlooking the 50 per cent more sailors required for his proposal of twenty-four conventional submarines, which, White claims, 'Australia could crew easily'); and the complete lack of detail on his own counter-policy (where are these supposed twenty-four conventional submarines coming from in the timeframe demanded?).

Along the way, the essay suggests that the Australian government plans to use SSNs to escort merchant ships. There is no evidence that the government plans this, nor would doing so make sense in terms of naval warfare and submarine operations (navies don't squander the incredible stealth of nuclear-powered submarines by having them tag along with easily found surface convoys). This is just one item from a list of contestable statements in the essay that is simply too long to address in this short rejoinder.

Indeed, that may be the strategy behind the argument: to overwhelm the reader with so many assertions that the other side of the debate is consumed with rebutting them all.

The lack of reference to government policy, or even to the work of other strategic analysts, is telling. Examination of speeches, policy documents, declarations of strategy, public capability plans, interviews with officials and politicians would not yield evidence in support of the assertion that the government is blindly, unreflectively and naively preparing to fight a war of aggression with China over Taiwan to preserve US primacy. Yet the essay paints a picture of a world of inevitable war – one that, it is claimed, the United States will most certainly lose: and AUKUS is *the* proof.

Such assertions keep the reader enthralled, but they do not inform actual policy. And ultimately that means White's piece does not serve the public by equipping them with the kind of evidence-based alternate strategies or difficult trade-offs that exist in the real world.

Peter J. Dean is the Director of Foreign Policy and Defence at the United States Studies Centre, University of Sydney, and was Co-Lead of the 2023 Defence Strategic Review Secretariat.

Justin Bassi

Hugh White's essay dismissing the AUKUS pact as a mistake takes the reader on a journey through everything that can go wrong and all the reasons we should never have been so ambitious. Unfortunately, it's a journey to nowhere, carefully bypassing the actual strategic vision of AUKUS, while concealing White's own central assumption that China will inevitably dominate the region, whatever Australia or any other country does.

White argues that Australia should do all we can to shape the region's future without ever describing what we should shape it into. This is a pattern for White, whose strategic argument tends to drop away at the critical moment. Thoughtful AUKUS advocates, by contrast, are quite clear about the strategy Australia is pursuing and how AUKUS fits into it. The goal is to shape a region in which power is balanced, rules and norms are observed or enforced, and China cannot wield untrammelled power to get what it wants, expanding its present malign behaviour, such as its aggression against other South China Sea claimants, its cyberattacks and its economic coercion.

White portrays this goal as an effort simply to preserve US dominance, even at the cost of a catastrophic war with China in which Australia would become entangled. Australia, he argues, is backing the wrong horse and should place its bets elsewhere.

But he is misrepresenting the end state that AUKUS supporters seek: not war for the United States but deterrence for an evolving and diverse region. White refuses to recognise that, as a regional power, Australia has agency and must contribute to a balance of the region that necessarily includes the United States – whose continued engagement should be encouraged through clear signals that others are prepared to step up.

The region is not defined by a simple contest between the United States and China. It is comprised of strong democracies such as Japan, India and South Korea, as well as South-East Asian nations like the Philippines that reject Beijing's bullying and are putting their security interests ahead of economic convenience.

Certainly, AUKUS faces challenges, which White dissects in detail. The submarine delivery and production schedules will be tough and the capability costs of slippage – always hard to avoid on such complex projects – could be high. Crewing will be difficult and some US lawmakers are airing concerns about their own submarine production capacity.

I can't address each of White's criticisms here, but largely his argument is that strengthening through partnerships is too hard and we should therefore submit. His fatalism doesn't allow for the fact that security cooperation between countries on something as significant as winning the global technology race needs a huge effort.

He is far too dismissive of AUKUS's Pillar Two, under which the three partners are working together on advanced military capabilities in areas such as artificial intelligence, quantum, cyber and hypersonics. Technological superiority confers military and strategic advantage; cooperation among like-minded democracies could make our capability development through advanced technologies greater than the sum of our parts. The gains can be increased by expanding Pillar Two to other nations, including Japan.

His cynical view that the United Kingdom is simply reviving its faded glory and chasing money from submarine construction ignores the demonstrably deeper cooperation that our two countries are pursuing, including through the British Royal Navy's increased regional presence and the treaty-level Defence and Security Cooperation Agreement announced by Australia and the United Kingdom in March 2024.

White acknowledges that nuclear-powered submarines are much faster and therefore better for operations beyond simply protecting Australia's northern approaches like crocodiles in a moat. A nuclear submarine can protect Australia but can also hunt enemy vessels in a sea battle north of the equator. That's a better warfighting capability, and therefore a better deterrent.

Despite White's dismissive attitude towards deterrence, sharper Australian teeth will help support the stability we need as our region evolves and we find ways to manage competition without conflict – or, if necessary, to be prepared for conflict.

His alternative – buying more cheaper conventional boats for the sole purpose of placing them to our north to defend our landmass – only makes sense if you agree with his strategy of letting the crisis come to us. That would mean accepting China as the dominant regional power – although he cloaks this by referring to "Asian great powers" – and then looking to merely survive, largely alone, what would no doubt be a grim period for our region. No United States, no AUKUS, no Quad, no Five Eyes, no hope.

Without our present partnerships – particularly the US alliance and the access it provides to intelligence and capabilities – the cost of defending Australia would become prohibitive. We would be weaker and have negligible regional influence. Those who value AUKUS recognise that Australia can thrive with our sovereignty, strategic choices and economic freedom intact, but only if we remain ambitious.

AUKUS is a challenge – I have no argument there. But as an assertion of military power, it's a tangible contribution, along with other partnerships, to upholding a favourable power balance and stability in our region. That will help create a safer neighbourhood, and will head off future crises, rather than waiting for them to come to our door while refusing the security of the best capability and best of friends.

Justin Bassi is Executive Director of the Australian Strategic Policy Institute. With over two decades of Australian Public Service experience, he was National Security Adviser to Prime Minister Malcolm Turnbull, including for the development of the 2016 Defence White Paper and selection of the Attack-class submarine, and was Chief of Staff to Foreign Minister Marise Payne, including during the time in which AUKUS was developed and announced.

Jennifer Parker

The decision to acquire nuclear-powered submarines represents a significant milestone in Australia's defence capability. Both the cost and the transition to a nuclear-powered capability in a country without a civilian nuclear industry warrants robust debate. There are pros and cons associated with the acquisition decision and its associated 'optimal pathway'. The core of the debate really centres on two elements. Is the opportunity cost of Australia's acquisition of nuclear-powered submarines worth the monetary and other costs? And can the risk be managed? On these two points, reasonable arguments can be progressed on either side.

Unfortunately, White's well-written, 46-page article does not progress the debate. White's argument, framed entirely in the negative, appears to misrepresent facts, to take liberties with assumptions represented as fact and to misunderstand key aspects of submarine employment and the requirements of a nation such as Australia that is an island dependent on maritime trade. An 800-word rebuttal cannot engage with all the issues with the piece, but I hope to encourage readers to cast a careful eye over its arguments. Here I focus primarily on some of the many problems with White's interpretation of maritime strategy and operations.

White is correct to suggest that Australia needs to articulate a strategy on which capability decisions are based, as I argued in my recent report, *An Australian Maritime Strategy: Resourcing the Royal Australian Navy*. However, he misunderstands essential elements of maritime strategy. For example, he suggests that an alternative to the acquisition of submarines could be to 'focus our defence closer to home, relying on a shallower but denser defensive shield'.

The obvious flaw in this argument is that Australia is a maritime nation: 98 per cent of our trade passes through the maritime domain, and 91 per cent of our fuel is imported, including all our aviation fuel to support the Royal Australian Air Force's F-35 operations, inevitably required to support White's suggested 'shallower defensive shield'. Why would an adversary attack Australia, when our trade – or, more accurately, our critical seaborne supply – is left undefended and ripe for the picking, as White suggests would be prudent? As the famed maritime strategist Alfred Thayer Mahan highlights, 'wars are won by the economic strangulation of the enemy from the sea', particularly wars against island nations.

White's misunderstanding of maritime strategy is underpinned by erroneous assertions that the defence of seaborne trade is no longer feasible. The explanation given for this bold but unjustified and unqualified statement is that 'technological trends … have made ships of all kinds easier to find and hit'.

Of course, as we have seen in the Red Sea, the proliferation of uncrewed explosive surface and aerial vehicles alongside anti-ship cruise missiles has increased the complexity of operations for warships in the littoral environment, which is the area of sea that can be influenced by threats from land. But unlike the Russian experience in the Black Sea, efforts of the United States and other allies and partners show that a well-defended ship with a well-trained crew can defeat these capabilities. As offensive capabilities evolve, so do counter-capabilities. This is the historical dance of naval warfare.

Quick to dismiss the value of nuclear-powered submarine operations, White suggests that the only argument put forward to support the need for Australia to acquire nuclear-powered submarines is the protection of maritime trade. It is not. The presence of unlocated nuclear-powered submarines significantly complicates an adversary's calculations and serves as a deterrent.

White's dismissal of the role of nuclear-powered submarines in the protection of maritime trade again misunderstands the fundamentals of maritime strategy and operations. White suggests that eight submarines cannot protect the 'over 17,000 voyages to Australian ports from overseas' and that submarines are 'very effective for attacking ships … but … not at all suited to defending them'. On the former: Australia does not need to protect all ships that visit Australian shores, it only needs to protect essential seaborne supply, comprising the fuel, ammunition and critical supplies that make up a much smaller subset of these voyages. On the latter: of course submarines will not be escorting ships along key trade routes. One look at Australian geography would show that carefully positioned submarines in the vicinity of key chokepoints would put at risk any adversary seeking to hold Australian seaborne supply at risk.

The length of this piece only permits a surface-level summary of some of the flaws in White's case against the delivery of AUKUS Pillar 1, of which there are many. While there are strong arguments for and against Australia's acquisition of nuclear-powered submarines, White's logic misunderstands the capability, its employment and the basic tenets of maritime strategy, and so must not be allowed to proceed unchallenged.

Jennifer Parker is an expert associate at the National Security College, Australian National University, and an adjunct fellow at the University of New South Wales in naval studies. She has over twenty years' experience in the Royal Australian Navy and specialised as anti-submarine warfare officer.

Justin Burke

In his polemic against AUKUS, Hugh White has once again shown himself to be a pithy and persuasive debater. Not to mention prolific – one might observe that if we were able to harness White's apparently limitless energy, we would not need nuclear propulsion for Australia's submarines. But we must score White, like all debaters, on both style and substance. On the former, he is undoubtedly skilled, if sometimes partial (witness how a commentator who agrees with him is a "renowned ... defence guru", while those who do not are mere "enthusiasts"). On the question of substance, readers must consider the following.

White is wrong when he states that "no government had seriously considered nuclear propulsion ... before the AUKUS plan was hatched", a claim easily disproven by research published by Sea Power Centre Australia, which shows it was first considered as early as 1959, and many times subsequently. The public record shows the option was still alive right up until 2019, when there was public discussion of the now-cancelled French Attack-class program transitioning to nuclear propulsion for the final few boats.

White is troublingly inconsistent when it suits his arguments. For example, he urges scepticism about Pillar 2, writing: "It is easy to talk up the military potential of exotic new technologies, but delivering real capabilities is a different matter." Later, he proposes that "uncrewed submarine drones" – a future technology covered by Pillar 2 – could replace our need for submarines and save the day. White as inadvertent advocate for the fruits of AUKUS Pillar 2 – who could have imagined?

Further, he states that the whole AUKUS plan may fail for the lack of just three crews of 120 Australian submariners, before arguing that his favoured plan of twenty-four conventionally powered boats – which would require 650 submariners, minimum – could be crewed "easily". Surely he cannot have it both ways.

Perhaps most egregiously, White dismisses out of hand the government's rare and significant disclosure that the practice of "snorting" (when conventional submarines approach the surface to run their diesel engines and charge their batteries) will become an unacceptable detection risk in the coming years. "[D]id the government suddenly learn, sometime between 2016 and 2021, of a dramatic and unexpected technological breakthrough in the detection of snorting conventional submarines?" he asks derisively, as if it could have happened any other way. He goes on to argue that this assessment should be disbelieved because other nations operating conventionally powered submarines have not apparently reacted; surely he is not suggesting that we ignore our own judgement and be the last to act?

A nuclear-powered submarine does not need to snort. But White argues that it is nuclear-powered submarines which will be detectable, citing a report published by the National Security College in 2020, which concluded that "the oceans are, in most circumstances, at least likely and, from some perspectives, very likely to become transparent by the 2050s". The report's own introduction described this prediction as "provocative" rather than definitive, and other reports published by the same institution as part of the same project had quite different conclusions. But to apply his yardstick above: should we not wait for the evidence of all other nations abandoning nuclear propulsion – or submarines altogether – before we believe this?

White is on stronger ground describing the huge challenges AUKUS will face in coming years, from the likely costs to the fragility of the United Kingdom's nuclear submarine enterprise and the uncertainties of the United States' political system. But where he sees reasons to capitulate now – a recurring theme in his oeuvre – most on the frontlines are emboldened by the significant successes of the past two and a half years, from persuading the famously risk-averse US nuclear navy that we could be trusted, to the tortuous but ultimately successful passage of key enabling legislation through the US Congress last year.

Let us be clear. White's prescription to return to square one and pursue another conventionally powered submarine fleet, which our own government believes would be detectable, is dangerous folly; even he concedes it "may prove impracticable", such that "our submarine capability collapses". It sounds eerily similar to our experience during World War II, when our nascent submarine fleet had lapsed due to cost, Sydney Harbour itself was penetrated by our enemy's subs and lives were lost. Readers are entitled to conclude that White's logic is flawed, that his alternative is no alternative at all, and that AUKUS – for all its challenges – is worth pursuing.

Justin Burke is a senior policy adviser at the National Security College, ANU, and a non-resident fellow at ISPK, Germany.

Christopher Skinner

In 'Fatal Shores', Hugh White sets out to demolish the tripartite AUKUS agreement. While the essay raises some of the mostly frequently discussed challenges, it fails to provide compelling evidence to support the predicted demise of the program.

The most important shortcoming is the proposition that the litany of failures in earlier endeavours of similar complexity is necessarily a harbinger of the future. On the contrary, each of the past failures is an object lesson in what not to do and in the pitfalls to avoid. The real problem is the unknown unknowns that will arise, and White is no more likely to predict those than any other mortal.

The essay begins by analysing the technologies within the second pillar of AUKUS, but casts doubt on whether the noble aim of synergistic collaboration will transpire for no other reason than that it will be difficult. If it were not, of course, no agreement would be necessary. This is especially so with nuclear propulsion for submarines, as Australia lacks experience in nuclear power generation or other applications of nuclear thermal energy.

Although White acknowledges the speed advantage of nuclear propulsion and the avoidance of the need to run diesel generators to recharge batteries, he asserts that a larger number of conventionally powered submarines for the same cost would be a better investment. This fails to comprehend that the superior mobility of nuclear submarines renders them a far greater threat. Coupled with their stealth, the much faster speeds of nuclear-powered subs makes their location in any area a matter of uncertainty.

White examines the increasing detectability of submarines, but this must be understood in context. A marginal risk of detection does not prevent the nuclear-powered submarine from performing its mission.

The essay then examines all the familiar saws on naval acquisitions and infers that this can never be improved. On the contrary, the vastly greater experience of the United States and the United Kingdom in major naval programs offers benefits to Australia that would not normally be available, except through consultancies of retired senior executives.

Perhaps White's most surprising statement is that the 'defence of seaborne trade is no longer operationally feasible. The only credible approach is to deter attacks on our trade by threatening attacks on an adversary's.' Yet the benefit of nuclear-powered submarines armed with ship and land-attack missiles is to threaten exactly that.

White also makes the mistake of assuming that a three-decade plan is set in concrete once announced – that somehow it cannot adapt to geopolitical and economic developments as it proceeds.

All complex programs evolve: it is wrong to assume that a change represents failure by some planner. On the contrary, a program like AUKUS will need to adapt frequently, and this should be expected and welcomed. The Submarine Rotational Force – West (SRF-W) may change if world events draw US and UK submarines to other theatres. The sale of three or more Virginia-class submarines to Australia may be forestalled by US Congressional or Department of Defense reassessment of priorities. And the SSN AUKUS development may be delayed by UK nuclear deterrent imperatives. But so what? These are all normal factors that arise in any long-term, large-scale program and will be dealt with just like any other major setback, such as that caused by intense weather.

The bottom line is that AUKUS has got off to an impressive start on its challenging journey, and will meet and overcome many obstacles along the way.

Christopher Skinner is a former naval engineer who was the initial project director for the ANZAC frigate program.

Josh Wilson

The argument about whether the AUKUS agreement to acquire nuclear-powered submarines was a good decision will continue, but there are no grounds for thinking the initial Morrison decision was well made. Margaret Simons' essay in Australian Foreign Affairs 19, "No Daylight", shows in the first paragraph how this entirely unsighted and momentous shift was announced and accepted in a flash. In Australian Foreign Affairs 20, Hugh White notes: "A good process does not always produce a good decision, but a bad process almost always produces a bad one." His argument that the AUKUS submarines are no exception to this rule is the most comprehensive and penetrating contribution of this kind to date.

Acknowledging at the outset that there has not been an appropriately searching public conversation about the largest defence acquisition in Australia's history, I nevertheless seek to challenge Jonathan Pearlman's statement that since Prime Minister Scott Morrison first uttered the "AUKUS" acronym on 15 September 2021, "there has been no political debate about this $368-billion decision". In any case, let me at add some detail and, I believe, daylight to the record.

On 18 October 2021, I spoke in the House of Representatives about the Morrison government's announcement:

> So the most important thing is that we ask questions and we expect answers, and that includes a number of questions that remain in relation to nuclear propulsion. Yes, nuclear submarines go faster and can remain submerged indefinitely from a propulsion point of view, but they're also noisier, with a more detectable heat signature because their cooling systems can never

switch off. They're also larger and less effective in coastal or littoral environments, which are characteristic of our region. They also cost more, with a larger crew complement, so inevitably you operate fewer submarines, and numbers do matter …

Even if the main game is ensuring that we have submarines that can go further and faster underwater for extended periods, the Australian public shouldn't think the choice is only between our existing diesel-electric propelled submarines and some yet to be determined nuclear option. A number of countries, including Japan and Germany, operate air-independent propulsion-based platforms, and the capability of these submarines is improving all the time. It's also a form of technology that much better suits our broader energy tech interests in future, and it will be more likely to be based on a genuine sovereign capability. Of course, it would avoid relying on the use of weapons-grade nuclear material, with the regional non-proliferation consequences of going down that path.

In any case, it's critical, in the aftermath of this government's submarine procurement disaster, that we don't get rushed down a particular path and that we don't allow the people who've made such a mess to dictate what happens next without proper scrutiny.

On 29 November 2021, the first parliamentary examination of the embryonic arrangement occurred through a Joint Standing Committee on Treaties inquiry, at which the head of the AUKUS Taskforce and other relevant departmental folk appeared.

I asked: "Has Defence or some other part of government formed an envelope with respect to the acceptable outside parameters, on the timeline and cost of the acquisition …?" (As it turned out, my attempt to pose a plainly unacceptable set of numbers – "sixty years and $500 billion" – was not far off the mark.) I also raised the non-proliferation consequences of having a nuclear-weapons state share weapons-grade fissionable material with a non-weapons state for the first time. Only *The Canberra Times* ran a story about the hearing.

The following day, in question time, Peter Dutton questioned my commitment to Australia's national security, suggesting that I was on the same page as the Russian and Chinese governments, and referring to me as "Comrade Wilson".

On 20 March 2023, in the week following the Albanese government's announcement of the details of the submarine acquisition, I made another parliamentary speech to say I was unconvinced that operating nuclear-powered submarines was in our strategic interest. I cited Allan Gyngell's concerns. I spoke about cost, complexity, nuclear waste and non-proliferation. I said:

> The AUKUS agreement, arrived at with some characteristically questionable secrecy by the former government, and some strange ministerial arrangements, is not a sports team of which we have all suddenly become life members. It is a significant partnership with two of our most important and closest allies, but it will only be effective if we do our job as parliamentarians, which is to look closely and ask questions in order to guard against risk.

Simons described the debate on the submarines at Labor's National Conference in August 2023 as "stage-managed". Again, while I do not argue that the outcome was somehow poised on a fine edge, I can say, as the seconder of Michael Wright's anti-AUKUS proposition, that it remained a fluid and free exercise up to and including that Thursday morning. It says a lot about the Labor Party's culture, and about the leadership of Anthony Albanese and Richard Marles, that both were happy to have the debate, and to lead their side of the case. The process by which the statement was considered prior to conference was open and robust, and resulted in substantial changes, one of which was quoted in White's piece.

Also notable and welcome is Defence Minister Richard Marles's acceptance of the recommendations of the "war powers" inquiry report in 2023. That will make a meaningful improvement to how the Parliament is engaged on defence and security decision-making, not least by creating a new committee that can consider classified material.

White's argument prompts us to ask whether there might be another fork in the road towards Australia's new submarines. And to consider how the AUKUS arrangement will actually unfold.

Based on everything we know about defence procurement, we should expect the submarine arrangement to involve considerable delays and additional costs. The life-of-type-extension process required for the Collins-class submarines will likely affect the hard-won acoustic signature of the boats, which is at the core of what has made them so formidable and will not be easy to maintain.

Australia is likely to experience an extended period in which our submarine coverage is substantially lent to us by rotating US boats, with perhaps a second-hand Virginia-class sub or two of our own. One reason to be wary of this prospect is the extent to which such an outcome might ultimately suit the US. Indeed, the "Background and Issues for Congress" paper produced by the Congressional Research Service includes a "potential alternative" to the proposed sale of Virgina-class SSNs to Australia, in which US SSNs would perform US and Australian missions, while Australia invested in forces for other missions for both Australia and the US. Since the appearance of White's piece, it has become clear that the US will not achieve what we understand to be the required production of two submarines per year.

Both White, in his use of Kurt Campbell quotes, and Elizabeth Buchanan, in her analysis of Australia's "pit stop" geography in Australian Foreign Affairs 20, present different reasons for us to drift towards a fundamentally borrowed and US-driven submarine capability.

From the beginning, my view has been that the most concerning issues with the AUKUS submarine arrangement are the strategic, sovereign capability and procurement risks. But we can't forget two further issues: first, that the regional balance and non-proliferation ramifications are serious and unresolved; and second, that the task of safely and permanently storing high-level nuclear waste has not been costed, nor is it even known to be technically feasible. There is no permanent storage repository for high-level nuclear waste anywhere on the planet, and neither the US nor the UK has fully decommissioned a single nuclear submarine, including boats that have been out of service for thirty years.

We have embarked on an excruciatingly long, complex, fraught and costly endeavour that, in my view, remains substantially unexplained and unjustified.

Josh Wilson is the Member for Fremantle in the Parliament of Australia.

Hugh White responds

I am grateful to the six people who have taken the trouble to respond in these pages to my essay on AUKUS in Australian Foreign Affairs 20, and for the chance to offer some thoughts in return. Let me start with the five responders who have written to defend AUKUS from my criticisms. To do that successfully, they would, I think, have to establish three propositions. They would need to argue, first, that SSNs would be more cost-effective in achieving Australia's key maritime operational objectives than conventional submarines. Second, that the AUKUS "optimal pathway" offers a credible plan to acquire and operate them. And third, that the wider strategic implications and commitments underpinning that plan are compatible with Australia's interests as the regional order evolves in the decades ahead.

We cannot expect a comprehensive argument for all three of these propositions, or even for any one of them, in the space available to AUKUS's defenders here. We could perhaps expect them to seek other opportunities to do so at whatever length is required to make their case properly. The need for this is clear, as no one inside or outside government has yet offered any serious defence of the plan. The result, as Peter Varghese has recently observed, is that while the arguments against AUKUS are now reasonably complex and sophisticated, the arguments in favour rarely rise above platitudes.

Nonetheless, the comments presented here offer valuable glimpses of the kinds of arguments that might be put forward in a serious attempt to defend AUKUS, so it might be helpful to offer some reflections on them.

Let's start with the relative cost-effectiveness of SSNs in meeting our operational objectives. Any discussion of this issue must start from a clear statement of what those objectives are. Jennifer Parker and Christopher Skinner both gesture in this direction by defending the idea that defence of trade is a – or the – primary operational priority for the RAN. I think that needs further argument: even though Australia depends heavily on trade, it makes no sense to say that defence of that trade is a key military priority unless military operations can effectively do so. That requires a credible "concept of operations" for this task.

Parker suggests one: stationing subs in the choke points through which our trade must pass. But a merchant ship is vulnerable throughout its voyage, so it must be protected continually, not just in choke points. It must also be defended from threats that subs cannot counter, like air-launched missiles. And even if we accept Parker's concept of operations, it still needs to be argued that the eight SSNs proposed under AUKUS would be more effective in her choke-point defence than the much larger number of conventional subs we could have for the same money. For reasons spelt out in my essay, the higher speed of SSNs alone does not ensure that. Nor does their uncertain advantage in stealth.

Justin Bassi suggests another operational role: that SSNs could "hunt enemy vessels in a sea battle north of the equator". True, but so can conventional subs, and, as I suggest in my essay, a lot more of them could sink a lot more ships in a lot more places than AUKUS's eight SSNs. That argument remains unanswered. And while it remains unanswered, there is no basis for claiming, as Bassi, Parker and Skinner all do, that SSNs provide a better deterrent. To support their case, they must argue convincingly that a small force of nuclear-powered subs would deliver a better operational outcome than a much larger fleet of conventional boats that are also easier to build, operate, crew and maintain – and that is very far from clear.

But is that bigger conventional fleet possible? Justin Burke and Peter Dean seem to think not. They see an inconsistency between my doubts that we will be able to crew Virginia-class subs under AUKUS and my confidence that we could crew a larger fleet of conventional subs. But the issues in each case are very different. There are two distinct reasons why we might be short of crews: a lack of recruits, and a lack of training opportunities. The crewing problem I foresee for AUKUS is the result of a lack of training opportunities. Because of delays in the Collins LOTE, the number of Collins-class subs available to go to sea will decline. That means that fewer and fewer trainees can gain the essential seagoing experience required to qualify for their roles and be ready to transfer to the Virginia-class subs, when or if they arrive. And the US Navy won't be able to offer enough training slots on their boats to solve our problem. They need all the seagoing training billets they can find to keep their own subs crewed.

We would have no problems maintaining a robust training pipeline if we managed to acquire a bigger fleet of conventional boats that provided plenty of seagoing training billets. Then our problem would be finding enough recruits to fill them. This is a serious challenge, but not insuperable. In my book *How to Defend Australia* (on pages 188–89, if you are interested), I offered a back-of-the-envelope estimate that to crew a fleet of conventional twenty-four subs, we would need to recruit 480 submariners a year from the 1.7 million Australians in the key recruiting age bracket of twenty to twenty-four. That doesn't sound impossible to me. The problem would be to maintain the training pipeline while we build that bigger conventional fleet. That is why I argue that we must move as fast as we possibly can to buy six 'off the shelf' subs from overseas.

Of course, that would be difficult, and so would the task of starting again from scratch to design and build a long-term replacement for the Collins subs. But would it be a harder and riskier path to a future submarine capability than the AUKUS plan? That brings us to the second of our questions. AUKUS advocates must explain why it make sense to bet on the 'optimal pathway' to deliver nuclear-powered submarines.

I'll confess to being a little surprised by the insouciant way that the responses here dismiss the many points of failure that loom in plain sight. Burke and Skinner, for example, both acknowledge the extraordinary risks. They draw confidence from what has been achieved so far, which seems a bold extrapolation from very modest preliminary steps, and they remain unperturbed by the mounting problems. Skinner, for example, admits that we might never get the Virginias, and that the British program might well be delayed. "But so what?" he asks. As an approach to risk management, this leaves a lot to be desired. He offers no thoughts as to how our submarine capability might be sustained under the AUKUS plan if the Virginias were not delivered. I do not see how it could be. He says there are risks in every project, which is true. But this is not a normal project, and these are not normal project risks.

The third question concerns the wider strategic implications of AUKUS. Plainly, it presupposes Australia's deep and enduring alignment with US strategic policy in our region, and specifically with its approach to China's challenge.

Much therefore depends on how successful that approach proves to be. The question is not whether we should prefer America to remain an active and effective counterbalance to Chinese power, but whether we can prudently assume that it will do so, as AUKUS does. I have argued at length elsewhere that I do not believe we can, for a fundamental reason: the costs and risks to America of confronting and containing a rival as powerful as China in China's own backyard outweigh the imperatives for America to do so. I have also argued that a failed attempt to do so carries a substantial risk of catastrophic war – a risk acknowledged by our leaders when they repeatedly say that we face the worst strategic circumstances since World War II. Advocates of AUKUS need to explain why they are so sure that US policy will work and that its dangers will be avoided. Simply saying that we must always support America because that's what we have always done in the past will not do, when we face such radically different circumstances.

Let me turn finally to Josh Wilson's commentary. Wilson has a special and important place in the AUKUS debate as the only federal parliamentarian from either major party to voice clear and cogent reservations about the plan, and a leading voice on the issue within the ALP. As he makes clear, the fruits of his efforts include the lively debate on AUKUS at last year's ALP National Conference, and he credits Anthony Albanese and Richard Marles for their willingness to engage in that process. But notwithstanding Wilson's efforts, Labor in government remains just as unshakably committed to the AUKUS plan as the Coalition, and as steadfastly resistant to explaining and defending this commitment in the face of growing doubts. Nor have the minor parties and independents sought seriously to challenge this toxic bipartisanship.

As a result, and for all the talk of Australia's "sovereign submarine capability", our government has completely surrendered control of the future of our submarine force. Its future will now be determined by decisions taken, and blunders committed, by people in Washington and London with interests and priorities very different from ours. It is good that Josh Wilson speaks out, but the fact remains that, on this issue at least, our system of government is simply not working.

Hugh White is an emeritus professor of strategic studies at the Australian National University.

Back Issues

ALL PRICES INCLUDE GST,
POSTAGE AND HANDLING.

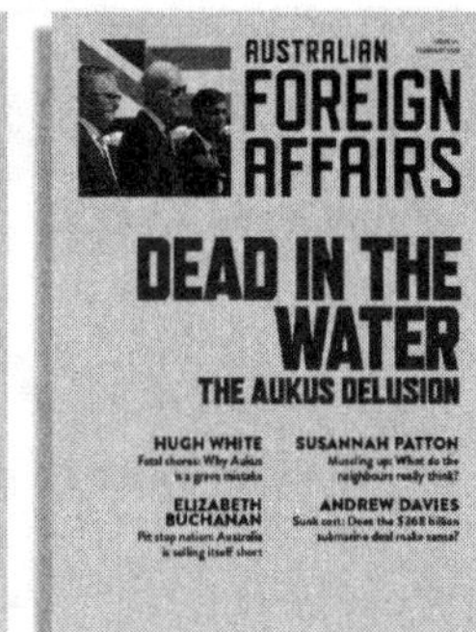

- ☐ **AFA3** ($19.99) Australia & Indonesia
- ☐ **AFA4** ($19.99) Defending Australia
- ☐ **AFA5** ($19.99) Are We Asian Yet?
- ☐ **AFA6** ($19.99) Our Sphere of Influence
- ☐ **AFA7** ($19.99) China Dependence
- ☐ **AFA8** ($19.99) Can We Trust America?
- ☐ **AFA9** ($19.99) Spy vs Spy
- ☐ **AFA10** ($19.99) Friends, Allies and Enemies
- ☐ **AFA11** ($19.99) The March of Autocracy
- ☐ **AFA12** ($19.99) Feeling the Heat
- ☐ **AFA13** ($19.99) India Rising?
- ☐ **AFA14** ($19.99) The Taiwan Choice
- ☐ **AFA15** ($22.99) Our Unstable Neighbourhood
- ☐ **AFA16** ($22.99) The Return of the West
- ☐ **AFA17** ($22.99) Girt by China
- ☐ **AFA18** ($22.99) We need to talk about America
- ☐ **AFA19** ($22.99) Does China really want to attack Australia?
- ☐ **AFA20** ($22.99) The AUKUS Delusion

PAYMENT DETAILS I enclose a cheque/money order made out to Schwartz Books Pty Ltd.
Or please debit my credit card (MasterCard, Visa or Amex accepted).

CARD NO. ☐☐☐☐☐☐☐☐☐☐☐☐☐☐☐☐

EXPIRY DATE / CCV AMOUNT $

CARDHOLDER'S NAME

SIGNATURE

NAME

ADDRESS

EMAIL PHONE

Post or fax this form to: Reply Paid 90094, Collingwood VIC 3066 **Freecall:** 1800 077 514 **or** +61 3 9486 0288
Fax: (03) 9011 6106 **Email:** subscribe@australianforeignaffairs.com **Website:** australianforeignaffairs.com
Subscribe online at australianforeignaffairs.com/subscribe (please do not send electronic scans of this form)

The Back Page

FOREIGN POLICY CONCEPTS AND JARGON, EXPLAINED

FRIENDSHORING

What is it: A method of avoiding trade and supply-chain disruption, in which countries trade with partners viewed as trustworthy or low-risk.

What isn't it: Friendshoring is different to "nearshoring", which involves favouring trade with nearby countries, and "onshoring", which involves basing manufacturing at home.

Who coined it: Following the outbreak of COVID-19, Bonnie Glick (former deputy administrator, USAID) proposed sourcing products from countries aligned with US interests – a move she labelled "allied-shoring". Adapting the term, Janet Yellen (secretary, US Treasury) in April 2022 referred to "friend-shoring", advocating trade with countries "we know we can count on".

Who likes it: Hugo Dixon (commentator-at-large, Reuters) has described it as a sensible way to avoid "putting all your eggs in one basket". Alberto Rizzi (fellow, EFCR) says friendshoring can promote climate action by reducing dependence on China, which dominates green technology supply chains.

Who doesn't: Raghuram G. Rajan (professor, University of Chicago) believes friendshoring fosters protectionism and makes war more likely between rivals such as the United States and China. Ngozi Okonjo-Iweala (director-general, WTO) warns that friends and enemies can quickly change, and that even friends can be unfriendly during trade: "Whenever someone proposes 'friend shoring', I always ask, 'Who is a friend?'"

Safer shores: Naoise McDonagh (lecturer, Edith Cowan University) says friendshoring can help countries respond to economic coercion, but that it should be called "safe-shoring" because the goal is "reducing dependence on high-risk nations, rather than only trading with formal allies or friends".